SIXTH EDI

EXPERIENCES IN
PUBLIC
SPEAKING

An Activity Book for Public Speaking

SPCH 1315

Marla D. Chisholm

Jackie Ganschow

Department of Communications
Del Mar College
Corpus Christi, Texas

Kendall Hunt
publishing company

All line art © Kendall Hunt Publishing Company.

Kendall Hunt
publishing company

www.kendallhunt.com
Send all inquiries to:
4050 Westmark Drive
Dubuque, IA 52004-1840

Dedication

This activity book is dedicated to ...

- our families who consistently support our efforts
- the DMC faculty who continue to be innovative in their teaching

Contents

Written Activities 81

Group Activities 111

Visual Aids 127

Researching 133

Informative Speaking 145

Persuasive Speaking 181

Additional Speaking Experiences 207

Feedback Forms 221

Preface to Public Speaking Students

As teachers who have taught communication classes for many years, we wanted to provide you with an activity workbook to enhance your public speaking experiences at Del Mar College.

You will find numerous oral, written, and group activities that will assist you in your growth process from a novice to a competent public speaker.

Since Del Mar is located on the Gulf Coast, we purposefully chose the whooping crane as our workbook "mascot." Just as our area is dedicated to the preservation of this magnificent bird, we, as teachers of communication, are dedicated to preserving the magnificent art of public speaking.

Marla D. Chisholm
Professor Emeritus

Jackie Ganschow
Professor Emeritus

Getting Acquainted with the Speech Communication Discipline

What Do We Offer at Del Mar College?

Course Description for SPCH 1315 from the Del Mar College Catalog

Introductory course in theories and practices of speech communication behavior in public speaking situations. Includes listener and audience analysis with an emphasis on research, organization, and delivery of informative and persuasive presentations. Pre-requisite: Successful completion of remedial English and Reading.

After completing this course, students will be able to meet the following competencies:

[1] Demonstrate speaking skills through an extemporaneous presentation that incorporates depth of research, orally cited sources, clear organizational pattern appropriate to topic and audience, visual aids, and effective verbal and nonverbal delivery skills.

[2] Demonstrate the ability to assess and improve presentational skills after receiving verbal, nonverbal, and written feedback.

[3] Demonstrate an understanding of the ability to orally apply basic principles of critical thinking and problem solving for purposes of argumentation.

Student Responsibilities

In order to meet these course objectives, all students will need to attend class regularly and make a time commitment outside of class. In all college courses, meeting course requirements will require more of a time commitment for some students than for others. Please understand that effort exerted will usually be reflected in the quality of the assignments completed, but remember that students are not graded on "effort." A student's grade will be the result of his or her performance on written assignments, oral presentations, exams, etc. Guidelines specified by the class instructor need to be followed, due dates need to be met, and information in the textbook and the activity book need to be understood and applied in presentations.

Ethical Behavior

Academic dishonesty will not be tolerated. One of the requirements for passing Public Speaking at Del Mar College is that students do their own work. You can receive an automatic "F" in the class for the semester if you have cheated and/or plagiarized on any written or oral assignment. You are expected to use ethical communication and behavior at all times, in all circumstances.

The Speech Faculty Offices

Full-time Speech faculty have individual office space in the Memorial Classroom Building in Room 103. Students should access instructors by their individual office phone numbers located on course syllabi.

The Communications, Languages, and Reading Department Office

The Speech discipline is part of the Communications, Languages, and Reading Department. Other disciplines in the department include: Radio/Television, Journalism, Languages, Reading, ESOL, and Freshman Seminar. Any concerns that cannot be addressed by your instructor or the Speech office staff can be brought to the attention of the department chairperson (698-1533). The office for the Communications, Languages, and Reading Department Chairperson is located in Room 134 in the Coles Building.

Speech Communication Center—SCC

The SCC aids all Del Mar students and faculty in the creation and performance of any speech activities. The SCC has personal computers, DVD/CD viewing equipment, and three practice rooms equipped with presentational equipment which clients can use to incorporate PowerPoint into their presentations, and cameras for persons to record themselves for self-analysis. Instructional recordings covering specific communication content areas give students the opportunity for additional clarification of information. Historical/political speech examples and Del Mar students' speeches are also available for viewing and critiquing. Clients can receive help from the lab consultants about speech organization, outlining, on-line research, visual aids, etc. The SCC is located in the Memorial Classroom Building in Room 211 and the phone number is 698-1581. Hours of operation may vary from semester to semester, so check with your instructor or the SCC staff.

Additional Opportunity in Speech Communication

Forensic Competition

Del Mar College is proud to provide a wonderful and unique opportunity to students through our nationally competitive forensic squad. The Vocal Viking Forensic Squad has been ranked nationally among community colleges and universities since 1998. Del Mar College is one of the few institutions of higher education in South Texas to provide this opportunity for students.

What is "forensics"? Many people think of forensic medicine or even forensic evidence in police detective work, but neither of these is close to forensic competition in the speech discipline. Forensic competition is competitive speech. The competition consists of Public Address events, Persuasive Speaking, After-Dinner Speaking, Extemporaneous, and Impromptu Speaking. Oral Interpretation events include Prose, Poetry, Drama, Duo, and a mixed genre event, Programmed Oral Interpretation.

Members of the squad work closely with the coach(es) in the events they choose and regularly travel to schools across the state and nation during the fall and spring semesters. The monetary cost of these trips is paid for by Del Mar College. The competitors pay with their time and dedication to the squad. In order to be a member of the Del Mar Vocal Viking Forensic Squad, you must be enrolled as a Del Mar student (required hours of enrollment vary) and maintain a G.P.A. of 3.0. In exchange for this, you will be able to travel to many college campuses, grow and mature as a student and citizen, meet wonderful people (both from your own team and other schools' teams), and HAVE FUN !!!!!

Other Speech Courses Offered at Del Mar College

SPCH 1311—Introduction to Speech Communication

A hybrid course, this class covers the theories and practice of speech communication behavior in interpersonal, small group, and public communication situations. The course introduces skills that students can use to communicate more effectively in their everyday lives. Students learn more about themselves, improve skills in communicating with others, and prepare and deliver formal public speeches. (3 hours freshman level credit)

SPCH 1318—Interpersonal Communication

In this class, students will learn and practice the communication skills needed throughout their personal and professional lives. This course is taught experientially, which means that participants are actively involved in exercises that emphasize the knowledge and practical understanding of the verbal and nonverbal dimensions of the communication process. Learn how to enhance your self-esteem; recognize how gender, class, ethnicity, age, and stereotypes impact our perceptions; understand the dynamics of your interpersonal relationships; learn to express emotions effectively; improve your listening skills; disclose your feelings and opinions without creating a defensive environment; express yourself assertively; and cope with your anger and/or frustration in conflict situations. (3 hours freshman level credit)

SPCH 1321—Business and Professional Communication

Anyone who wants to communicate more effectively on the job can benefit from this course. Business and Professional Communication is designed to improve communication skills at work or in organizational settings. You will learn what makes on-the-job communication effective and also which behaviors are ineffective or even destructive in the workplace. Learn how to research and deliver individual and group oral presentations, choose the best decision-making method, respond constructively and professionally to an appraisal of your job performance, encourage each person's participation in group meetings, strengthen your ability to implement win-win negotiating style, improve your accuracy in listening, and identify your own nonverbal behaviors that help and hinder your effectiveness on the job. (3 hours freshman level credit)

SPCH 2333—Discussion and Small Group Communication

Working effectively in groups is an essential part of everyone's work and social experience. This course is designed for anyone interested in improving his or her group skills. Learn how to work together successfully, utilize critical thinking skills in a small group setting, emulate valuable leadership skills, put group problem-solving into action, run a successful meeting, and identify and demonstrate conflict management skills. (3 hours sophomore level credit—course offered on a rotating basis)

SPCH 2341—Oral Interpretation

Oral Interpretation is a popular class at colleges and universities nationwide. It is a course in which prose, poetry, and drama come alive through a performer's verbal and non-verbal interpretation of the literature. This class can be particularly valuable for education majors who will be reading aloud to children, for English majors with a zest for understanding literary works, for speech and drama majors who want to work on characterization and voice, and for any person who loves to hear the written word jump from the page to the imagination. (3 hours sophomore level credit—course offered on a rotating basis)

Why Not Double Major?

Benefits of adding a speech degree to your academic plan

Many students believe that a degree in speech means taking a lot of classes where you have to speak in front of the class. While this is an important skill, and some speech classes do have this component, some speech classes do not. Speech degrees include classes like: Interpersonal Communication (one-on-one), Small Group Communication (leadership and team building), Business Communication (interviewing skills), Rhetoric (the study of speeches), Nonverbal Communication, and many more.

Think about your declared major. Aren't "communicating well with co-workers," "leadership qualities," "team building," "the ability to react appropriately," and "conflict management" all qualities that could benefit you in your job? Of course they are!

Del Mar College is an excellent school with very affordable prices. Why not double-major here? When you double-major, you will receive a degree in two different areas, but it only requires an additional 15–18 hours! Those hours will transfer into your bachelor's degree—one as your major, and the other as your minor. That means you really aren't spending more time or money—it is simply a matter of where you spend that time and money!

See the diagram on the next page which illustrates how double-majoring at Del Mar will work into your Bachelor Degree program. It works!

**The diagram on the next page is a generic one. Some degree plans have specific minors to accompany their majors, but you would still have an Associate Degree in Speech about which you can boast!

**Most Universities will also have a language requirement. You may complete that requirement at Del Mar as well.

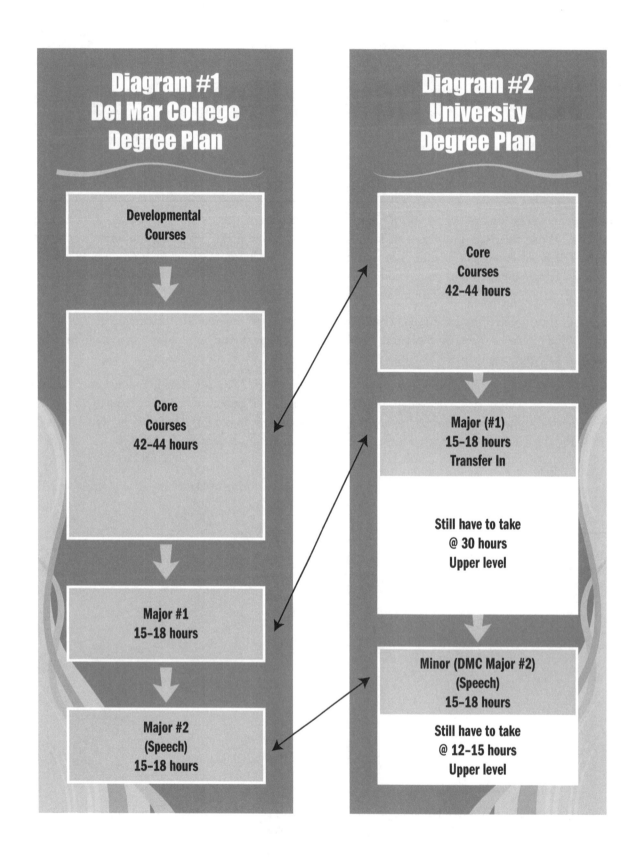

Diagram #1
Del Mar College
Degree Plan

Developmental Courses

Core Courses 42–44 hours

Major #1 15–18 hours

Major #2 (Speech) 15–18 hours

Diagram #2
University
Degree Plan

Core Courses 42–44 hours

Major (#1) 15–18 hours Transfer In

Still have to take @ 30 hours Upper level

Minor (DMC Major #2) (Speech) 15–18 hours

Still have to take @ 12–15 hours Upper level

Speech 1315   Name _____

Fall/Spring/Summer I/II/May   Preferred Name: _____

Date: _____   Class Time: _____

Student Information Sheet

Telephone: (home) _____

       (cell) _____

E-Mail address: _____

Student ID Number: _____

Major: _____

Ultimate career goals/occupational plans: _____

_____

Approximate number of completed college credit hours: _____

Previous Speech/Communication Courses: _____

List three topics on which you might be interested to speak.

_____

_____

What is your absolute worst fear about speaking in public?

_____

Please share anything else you think your instructor ought to know about you.

_____

_____

Student Validation Form

SPEECH 1315—Public Speaking is a freshman level course with a prerequisite that any required remediation courses in English and Reading need to be successfully competed prior to enrollment.

Signing this form indicates that:

I understand the prerequisite for this course.

I have also read and understood the SPCH 1315 course policies which include attendance requirements and grading procedures. This information has been provided in the course syllabus given to me by my instructor at the beginning of the semester.

I understand that I am expected to put my best effort into my work and to spend a significant amount of time outside of the classroom on course assignments.

I also understand the policy regarding ethical standards and the consequences for failing to meet these standards.

Student Signature _____

Print Name _____

Instructor _____

Class Time _____

Date _____

Criteria for Grading Speeches

The following guidelines are established by the National Communication Association, an organization dedicated to speech education. The criteria are used as guidelines in public speaking classes throughout the country and will be used by your instructor to evaluate your informative and persuasive speeches.

To receive a **C** on your speech, you must meet the following standards:

[1] The speech must be original.

[2] The type of speech presented must be appropriate to the assignment.

[3] The topic must be sufficiently focused and appropriate for the audience.

[4] The speech must fit the time requirements of the assignment.

[5] The speech must be presented on the day assigned.

[6] Main ideas must be supported with facts, figures, appropriate testimony, examples, or narratives.

[7] The speech must have a clear sense of purpose.

[8] The speech must have a clearly identifiable and appropriate design, complete with an introduction and conclusion.

[9] The speech must be presented extemporaneously.

[10] The speech must satisfy any specific requirements of the assignment, such as number of references, formal outline, or use of visual aids.

[11] The speaker must use language correctly.

To receive a **B** on your speech, you must meet the following standards:

[1] Satisfy all requirements for a *C* speech.

[2] Select a challenging topic and adapt it appropriately to your audience.

[3] Reflect a greater depth of research.

[4] Clearly identify sources of information and ideas.

[5]   Create and sustain attention throughout the speech.

[6]   Make effective use of transitions, previews, and summaries.

[7]   Use good oral style.

[8]   Present your speech with poise.

To receive an *A* on your speech, you must meet the following standards:

[1]   Satisfy all requirements of a *B* speech.

[2]   Demonstrate imagination and creativity in topic selection and development.

[3]   Develop and sustain strong bonds of identification among the speaker, audience, and topic.

[4]   Consistently adapt information and supporting material to the experiential world of your audience.

[5]   Reflect an even greater depth of research.

[6]   Demonstrate artful use of language and stylistic techniques.

[7]   Make a polished presentation that artfully integrates verbal and nonverbal communication skills.

A *D* speech does not meet one or more of the standards for a *C* speech or

[1]   It is obviously unrehearsed.

[2]   It is based entirely on biased information or unsupported opinions.

An *F* speech does not meet three or more of the standards of a *C* speech, reflects either of the problems associated with a *D* speech, or

[1]   It uses fabricated supporting material.

[2]   It deliberately distorts evidence.

[3]   It is plagiarized.

Peer Critiquing

Critiquing is the art of evaluating or analyzing a speech. Students should learn to expect feedback about their speeches and accept it with a receptive attitude. Actual practice in the evaluation of speeches can aid you in finding examples, both good and bad, of the criteria which are taught in a public speaking class.

Your Responsibility as a Speech Critiquer

When someone speaks, the assumption, although sometimes faulty, is that someone else is listening. Listening, then, is actually the counterpart of speaking. Certainly in the public speaking process there is no speech without listeners. The listener is one-half of the entire communication process.

In order to fulfill your responsibilities as an audience member in this course, you will be learning and practicing the skill of critical listening. Critical listening means using your abilities and skill to better evaluate the content, organization, language, and delivery of a speaker's presentation.

Since feedback is the primary means by which we learn to improve, especially in the classroom, the specific judgments you make about speech content and delivery need to be presented effectively to the speaker. Commit yourself to becoming the most effective listener you can be. By doing so, you will become a more effective speaker.

Characteristics of Good Critiquing

[1] It is objective. If you make a subjective statement, clearly identify it as such. For example, saying "I thought you were dressed professionally" is better than saying "Your dress is pretty."

[2] It is definite. Avoid "I'm not sure, but …" Also avoid generalized comments like "Your eye contact was poor," or "You messed up on your visual aid." Say instead, "You often looked at the back wall" or "Your PowerPoint slides didn't have consistent capitalization."

[3]   It is understandable (organized).

[4]   It is **constructive** and helpful.

[5]   It contains praise as well as suggestions for improvement. If you point out a flaw, give a constructive alternative. Saying "Don't be nervous" is not as helpful as saying "Avoid scratching your nose and straightening your collar."

[6]   It avoids ridicule, sarcasm, and intimidation.

[7]   It evaluates the **important** aspects of the speech and does not dwell on the minor ones. One "uh" or a passing glance at the back wall is not worth mentioning.

[8]   It is the evaluation of a single effort, not a general overall evaluation of past speeches or general speech skills.

Ice Breakers

Get to Know You

Objective

To begin to learn one another's names and some unique facts about each other.

Instructions

- You must ask a classmate if he/she fills a particular category.
- You write his/her name in the blank on your sheet.
- Don't volunteer information!
- Try to get as many different names as possible on your sheet.
- Have fun!

[1] _____ Played a high school sport.

[2] _____ Listens to classical music.

[3] _____ Has never changed a diaper.

[4] _____ Has traveled overseas.

[5] _____ Has met someone famous.

[6] _____ Is a parent.

[7] _____ Has had more than four jobs.

[8] _____ Was born in another state or country.

[9] _____ Is left handed.

[10] _____ Plays a musical instrument.

[11] _____ Sleeps with a stuffed animal.

[12] _____ Is married.

[13] _____ Got a speeding ticket in the last six months.

[14] _____ Knows how to change the oil in a car.

[15] _____ Is unemployed.

[16] _____ Has a living great-grandparent.

[17] _____ Likes to eat cold pizza for breakfast.

[18] _____ Has been on television.

[19] _____ Cries during sad movies.

[20] _____ Is in love.

Name _____

Partner's Name _____

My New Best Friend

Objective

To meet and introduce one of your classmates.

Instructions

Use the following questions to interview your "new best friend." When you introduce him/her, begin by saying, "This is _____, my new best friend." Share the information you have learned from this interview with the rest of the class.

How long have you lived in South Texas? _____

What do you do to pay the bills? _____

If money were no object, what would your dream career be? _____

What would your best friend say is unique about you? _____

_____

You can't tell by **looking** at you that _____

_____

With what communication skill would a family member say you could use some help?

Name of person/relationship to you: _____

Skill: _____

What are some ways that you deal with stress? _____

_____

What is your favorite "comfort food"? _____

Credibility and Public Speaking

Gaining and Maintaining Credibility in Public Speaking Presentations

Credibility is the audience's perception of a speaker's competence, trustworthiness, and dynamism. Your listeners (*not you*) determine whether you have or lack credibility. Regardless of how they feel about your topic, if audience members regard you as credible, they will be much more likely to be interested in and receptive to what you have to say.

Speakers have the opportunity to enhance their credibility (ethos) in three phases; initial, derived, and terminal.

Initial Credibility/Ethos

Your audience forms this perception before you begin to speak. It is based on:

- Your reputation
- The manner in which you approach the speaking area
- Your appearance and grooming
- Your posture, facial expression, eye contact, and poise

Derived Credibility/Ethos

Your audience forms this perception as you present yourself and your message. Consider these skills for enhancing your credibility as you speak:

- Tell your audience your link to or expertise with your topic
- Establish common ground with your audience
- Support your main points with research
- Cite all sources of information with oral citations
- Define all terms for your audience (don't assume they already know)
- Use appropriate language
- Avoid verbal fillers, gender-biased language, slang, and profanity
- Show enthusiasm/sincerity in delivery

Terminal Credibility/Ethos

Your audience forms this perception when you have finished your speech. Consider these tips:

- Maintain eye contact when ending your speech
- Finish speaking, pause, and then gather up your materials—visuals, note cards, etc.
- Maintain poise as you walk to your seat

What Do I Wear for a Speech?

Do wear

- Appropriate clothing for the speech topic
- Clothes that fit (not oversized or too tight)
- Clothes that are clean and ironed
- Shirts (tucked in if designed to be)
- Shirts with sleeves
- Belt (if pants have belt loops)
- Shoes
- Hair away from eyes and face

Don't wear

- Clothes with tears or holes
- Low-cut jeans (we don't want to see your belly button or your boxer shorts)
- Short shorts or very short skirts
- Tops revealing midriff or cleavage
- Halter tops
- See-through tops
- T-shirts with logos, slogans, or irrelevant, distracting pictures/writing
- Outerwear (caps, hats, or coats)
- Sunglasses on your face or on top of your head
- Jewelry that is oversized, noisy, or clunky
- Distracting piercings
- Flip-flops or other very casual footwear

Cover up

- Large or distracting tattoos, if possible

Remember—Your appearance has a significant impact on your initial credibility. You may lose points on your speech grade if you dress inappropriately.

Unethical Behavior: Determining Plagiarism and Cheating

Objective

To recognize unethical behavior when it occurs in a Public Speaking course.

Instructions

After reading about the three different kinds of plagiarism, analyze the situations given below and decide if the students have committed plagiarism or have cheated. If you think the students have plagiarized, identify which kind of plagiarism they committed. Be able to defend your decisions orally.

> To **plagiarize** is to present another person's language or ideas as your own—to give the impression that you have written or thought of something yourself when you have actually taken it from someone else.
>
> **Global plagiarism:** stealing an entire speech or assignment
>
> **Patchwork plagiarism:** stealing ideas or language from two or three sources
>
> **Incremental plagiarism:** failing to give credit for particular parts or increments of a speech that are borrowed from other people (quotes or paraphrases)

[1]   Anna buys an entire speech from an online source, writes it on note cards, and then delivers it as if it were her own work.
Anna (has) (has not) plagiarized. Reasons?

[2]   On the Internet, Aiden finds an outline of a speech about college students and stress. He adds one additional example to the speech, but otherwise does not change it. Aiden then presents the speech in class as his own.
Aiden (has) (has not) plagiarized. Reasons?

[3]   Ruben and Matthew are in two different Public Speaking sections. They work together on a speech on the topic of "How the Pyramids Were Built." They share the same sources: two Internet sources and a book. They write the speech together and prepare identical outlines. Each gives essentially the same speech in his class.
Ruben and Matthew (have) (have not) cheated. Reasons?

[4] Vivian uses statistics extensively in her speech on medical waste which washes up on local beaches, but she does not tell her audience the sources of her statistics.
Vivian (has) (has not) plagiarized. Reasons?

[5] Together, Monica and Alex watch two instructional DVDs in the SCC. Monica completes the worksheets that accompany the DVDs, but Alex doesn't find the time. He copies Monica's worksheets and turns them in for credit.
Alex (has) (has not) plagiarized. Monica (has) (has not) cheated. Reasons?

[6] Together, Becky and Audrey watch two instructional DVDs in the SCC. After watching the recordings, they work together on the worksheets that accompany the DVDs. They turn in identical worksheets.
Becky and Audrey (have) (have not) cheated. Reasons?

[7] Together, Jack and David watch two instructional DVDs in the SCC. After watching the DVDs, they discuss the answers to the worksheets that accompany the recordings. Later that day, each one individually completes the worksheets.
Jack and David (have) (have not) cheated. Reasons?

[8] Ian's class is expected to watch a recorded speech in the SCC and write a critique on the speech. Ian doesn't watch the speech, but his friend Marco does. Ian takes Marco's critique and rewrites it. Ian makes sure to vary the sentence structure and the wording so that the critique is not identical to Marco's.
Ian (has) (has not) plagiarized. Marco (has) (has not) cheated. Reasons?

[9] Amanda finds three articles online that each offer unique information about her speech topic. She uses pieces of all three articles when she writes her speech. The day of her speech she does not cite any of these sources, although she does cite some other sources from which she gathered information.
Amanda (has) (has not) plagiarized. Reasons?

[10] Leslie and Reid, who are in different Public Speaking classes, are working in the SCC on an assignment that requires them to make a slide show for a PowerPoint presentation. Leslie doesn't know much about PowerPoint, so Reid helps her. He explains how to download photos and shows her a picture he has downloaded from the Internet that he intends to use for his assignment. Interestingly, Leslie realizes that this same picture would be appropriate for her presentation also. She downloads the identical picture and uses it in her slide show.
Leslie (has) (has not) cheated. Reasons?

[11] Jose and Sarah are in the same Public Speaking class. Jose finds an Internet source that has interesting information for Sarah's topic area. He gives Sarah the web address, and she gets valuable information from the site. Sarah uses the source in her speech even though she did not find it on her own.
Jose and Sarah (have) (have not) cheated. Reasons?

[12] Lillian, Noah, Ramesh, and Courtney form a study group. When a take-home test is distributed in their Public Speaking class, all four of the students make sure they have read the chapters and studied for the test. At a set time, they meet to collaboratively take the test.
The students in the study group (have) (have not) cheated. Reasons?

Oral Activities

Self-Items Introduction (2–3 Minutes)

Objectives

1) To give you the opportunity to speak in a non-threatening format, 2) to briefly relate information about yourself so other class members will be better acquainted with you, 3) to ease some of the initial speech anxiety felt in the class.

Instructions

[1] Choose two objects that represent or symbolize significant information about yourself. Examples: people close to you, activities with which you are associated, your ambitions, your talents, or anything else you think is an important part of your "self."

[2] The objects that you choose can be ordinary objects found around your home or outdoors. Remember to give some thought to your choices. Your fellow class members do not (as of yet) know you. What you share at this early stage in the semester makes a strong impression.

[3] Jot down the reasons you chose the objects and what each "says" about who you are and how you feel about yourself and your life.

[4] Read over your notes and decide what you want to share with the class. Then, on index cards, write down a few key words to jog your memory while you deliver your speech.

[5] Give some thought on how you are going to begin. Start your presentation creatively. **DON'T SAY,** "My name is _____ and the first object I brought is _____." You could, instead, begin by saying, "On first glance you may overlook me because I'm quiet and don't usually initiate conversations, but the real me is extremely sensitive and very organized. This shell and planner notebook symbolize these qualities."

[6] To conclude, DON'T SAY "That's it … that's me … I don't have anything else to say." Clearly and creatively make a statement letting your audience know you are finished. You could, for example, say, "So don't be fooled by your first impressions. Take the time to recognize my strengths and get to know me better." After you have finished speaking, pause briefly before you return to your seat.

[7] To understand the criteria by which your grade will be based, review the Self-Items Introduction Evaluation on the following page.

[8] Practice your presentation point by point (not word for word) until you can deliver the information with only occasional glances at your notes. Know your introductory statement very well.

[9] When it is time to give your presentation, give your signed Self-Items Introduction Evaluation to your instructor. This form will be used to critique and grade your presentation. Go to the front of the room, pause, then begin. Look directly at your audience while speaking. Smile. Glance at your notes only on occasion—just long enough to pick up the cue for your next item. Speak in a natural conversational style, as if you were talking to a group of friends.

Name _____

Class Time _____

Self-Items Introduction Evaluation

To be filled out by instructor:

MISSING	POOR	FAIR	GOOD	EXCELLENT
0 pts.	1–4 pts.	5–6 pts.	7–8 pts.	9–10 pts.

[1] The content of your presentation revealed how your objects were representative of important information in your life. _____ pts.

[2] You began your presentation in a creative manner. _____ pts.

[3] Your material showed prior thought and preparation. _____ pts.

[4] You had a clear and creative conclusion. _____ pts.

[5] You presented your self-items with enthusiasm/sincerity. _____ pts.

[6] You looked at the audience most of the time. _____ pts.

[7] You used natural gestures and good posture. _____ pts.

[8] Your face was expressive. _____ pts.

[9] You wrote your notes on note cards. _____ pts.

[10] You adhered to time requirements/restrictions _____ pts.

TOTAL POINTS = GRADE _____

Comments:

Self-Introduction Activity

Complete the following items and prepare to present this information in a
conversational format.

What is your name? _____

By what name do you prefer to be called? _____

Where were you born? _____

Where did you grow up? _____

Are you currently employed? _____

    Where do you work? _____

    What type of work do you do? _____

    What type of work have you done in the past? _____

Why are you attending Del Mar College? (Major, Goals, etc.)

_____

_____

What are three things you really like?

[1] _____

[2] _____

[3] _____

What are three things you really dislike?

[1] _____

[2] _____

[3] _____

Of what in your life are you most proud?

_____

_____

Complete the statement:
"You would never know from looking at me that …"

_____

_____

Me in a Minute

Objectives

1) To ease some of the initial tension felt in the class, **2**) to give you the opportunity to speak in a non-threatening format, **3**) to briefly (one minute) relate information about yourself so other classmates will be better acquainted with you.

Instructions

[1]   Choose two adjectives that you feel best describe you. Be sure they reveal significant information about you—words you think are an important description of your "self." Examples might be: artistic, athletic, gregarious, musical, aggressive, or studious. Remember to give some thought to your choices. Your fellow classmates do not (as of yet) know you. What you share at this early stage in the semester makes a strong impression.

[2]   Jot down the reasons you chose these words and what each "says" about who you are and how you feel about yourself and your life. You might even think of an example or a story from your life that illustrates your two descriptive words.

[3]   Read over your notes and decide what you want to share with the class. Remember that you only have one minute to speak! On index cards, write down a few key words to jog your memory while delivering your speech.

[4]   Plan your *grabber*. Start your presentation creatively. **Don't say,** "My name is _____ and two words that describe me are handsome and scatterbrained." Say instead, "Until I made two hundred dollars for modeling suits at a recent men's fashion show, I never would have described myself as handsome. However, if I can make that kind of money for a couple of hours' work, I'll believe the agency that hired me!" (Of course, you would also have to explain the "scatterbrained" part in your speech.)

[5]   To conclude, **don't say,** "That's it, that's all I have to say" or "That's me. I'm done." Every speech must have a *clincher*. That is a creative statement that lets the audience know you are finished.

[6]   Practice this oral activity point by point (not word for word) until you can deliver the information with only occasional glances at your notes. Know your grabber very well.

[7]   When it is your turn to speak, go to the front of the room, pause, and then begin. Look directly at your audience while speaking. Smile. ☺ Glance at your notes just long enough to pick up the cue for your next item. Speak in a natural conversational style, as if you were talking to a group of friends.

[8]   After you have finished speaking, pause briefly before you return to your seat.

[9]   Remember, **all of your classmates and your professor want you to succeed!**

Tongue Twisters and Articulation Drills

[1] How can a clam cram in a clean cream can?

[2] I saw Susie sitting in a shoe-shine shop. Where she sits she shines, and where she shines she sits.

[3] The thirty-three thieves thought that they thrilled the throne throughout Thursday.

[4] Something in a thirty-acre thermal thicket of thorns and thistles thumped and thundered threatening the three-D thoughts of Matthew the thug. Although, theatrically, it was only the thirteen thousand thistles and thorns through the underneath of his thigh that the thirty-year-old thug thought of that morning.

[5] Can you can a can as a canner can can a can?

[6] Roberta ran rings around the Roman ruins.

[7] Six sick hicks nick six slick bricks with picks and sticks.

[8] I wish to wish the wish you wish to wish, but if you wish the wish the witch wishes, I won't wish the wish you wish to wish.

[9] Stupid superstition!

[10] There was a fisherman named Fisher who fished for some fish in a fissure. 'Til a fish with a grin, pulled the fisherman in. Now they're fishing the fissure for Fisher.

[11] World Wide Web

[12] Picky people pick Peter Pan Peanut-Butter, 'tis the peanut-butter picky people pick.

[13] If Pickford's packers packed a packet of crisps would the packet of crisps that Pickford's packers packed survive for two and a half years?

[14] Six sleek swans swam swiftly southwards.

[15] When you write copy you have the right to copyright the copy you write. You can write good and copyright, but copyright doesn't mean copy good. It might not be right good copy, right?

[16] How much wood could Chuck Woods' woodchuck chuck, if Chuck Woods' woodchuck could and would chuck wood? If Chuck Woods' woodchuck could and would chuck wood, how much wood could and would Chuck Woods' woodchuck chuck? Chuck Woods' woodchuck would chuck, he would, as much as he could, and chuck as much wood as any woodchuck would, if a woodchuck could and would chuck wood.

[17] Rolling red wagons

[18] When I was in Arkansas I saw a saw that could outsaw any other saw I ever saw, saw. If you've got a saw that can outsaw the saw I saw saw then I'd like to see your saw saw.

[19] He threw three balls.

[20] We're real rear wheels.

[21] I wish to wash my Irish wristwatch.

[22] How many sheets could a sheet slitter slit if a sheet slitter could slit sheets?

[23] Silly sheep weep and sleep.

[24] Truly rural, truly rural, truly rural.

[25] Round and round the rugged rock the ragged rascal ran.

[26] Mo mi mo me send me a toe,
Me me mo mi get me a mole,
Mo mi mo me send me a toe,
Fe me mo mi get me a mole,
Mister kister feet so sweet,
Mister kister where will I eat?

Name _____

Class Time _____

Audience Analysis Presentation—"The Commercial"

Objective

To effectively adapt a topic for a particular audience and situation.

Instructions

[1]   Read text material on audience analysis. On the assigned date you may be asked to bring to class a wrapped (new) item, or this item might be provided by your instructor. The item must perform a function—it has to do something. Examples of items that <u>do not</u> meet this "function" requirement are: stickers, food, newspaper, poster, or money. Examples of items that <u>do</u> meet this function are: pen, flashlight, rolling pin, or clothes hanger. If you are required to bring an item, be creative in choosing it. Do not bring inappropriate or embarrassing items.

[2]   Anyone who forgets and fails to bring his/her wrapped item on the assigned date, or does not have an item assigned to him/her by the instructor, will not have the opportunity to participate in the activity (receiving a "0" for the assignment).

[3]   You will be choosing an audience provided by your instructor. You will then select a wrapped item (other than your own) from the "gifts" brought by the class or from the items provided by your instructor.

[4]   Create a commercial that will sell this item to your specific audience. For example, you might have to sell a flashlight to an audience comprised of skydivers or sell a clothes hanger to birdwatchers. Be sure to spend time analyzing how you will develop your commercial to meet the particular needs and interests of your target audience.

[5]   Do not give your item magical qualities. For example, your item cannot take pictures (unless it's a camera), or it doesn't magically contain a microphone or a computer chip. You need to work with the item you have.

[6]   Look at the design of your item and come up with two functions for the item (beyond its original function). Those two functions need to meet the needs of the specific audience that you have been assigned. For example, you cannot sell a garlic press to a group of plumbers because they like Italian food like everyone else likes Italian food. You need to sell the item not merely as a garlic press but with two functions that will aid your audience of plumbers to meet their needs, make more money, satisfy customers, etc.

[7]   Give your item a name. Product names will help you get objectives, and keep your audience's attention and make your product more marketable.

[8]   Demonstrate your item if you can. If it is in a package, take it out and make sure your audience can see it. If you need to bring something else with you to demonstrate what your item can do, that is acceptable.

[9]   Stretch your imagination! One criteria on which you will be evaluated is your creativity. Make sure that you clarify what you want your particular audience to know, understand, and appreciate about your item. Clarify how your item is different from others that look just like it. Convince this audience that it will be in their best interest to buy the item.

[10] Begin the commercial with an attention getter. Ask a question, begin with a quote, or start with a hypothetical example. Another option as your attention getter for this oral activity is to give yourself credibility as the inventor of the item. For instance, you can be a plumber yourself or the owner of a very successful plumbing business.

[11] Deliver your commercial extemporaneously. You can use note cards; just don't read to your audience. Be enthusiastic and passionate about your product.

[12] Use your time to complete all the objectives on the grade form in this activity book. Usually a commercial is 30–60 seconds. No infomercials, please.

[13] Dress appropriately to add to your credibility.

[14] Fill out the top student portion of the Audience Analysis Evaluation. On the assigned date, turn in the signed evaluation form to your instructor before delivering your commercial. This form will be used to critique and grade your oral activity.

Name _____

Class Time _____

Audience Analysis Evaluation

To be completed by student:

ACTUAL ITEM: _____

YOUR MADE-UP PRODUCT NAME: _____

AUDIENCE: _____

To be completed by instructor:

MISSING	POOR	FAIR	GOOD	EXCELLENT
0 pts.	1–4 pts.	5–6 pts.	7–8 pts.	9–10 pts.

[1]   You addressed the needs and interests of your specific target audience. _____ pts.

[2]   You clarified what is special/unique about your item so that your audience REALLY wants to purchase it. _____ pts.

[3]   You "grabbed" your audience's attention within your first few statements. _____ pts.

[4]   Your material showed prior thought and preparation. _____ pts.

[5]   Your material showed creativity. _____ pts.

[6]   Your item has two functions beyond its original functions _____ pts.

[7]   You used good eye contact and extemporaneous delivery. _____ pts.

[8]   You used vocal variety. _____ pts.

[9]   Your gestures and movement were natural. You demonstrated your item if possible. _____ pts.

[10] You were dressed appropriately enhancing your credibility. _____ pts.

TOTAL POINTS = GRADE _____

Comments:

Speech Communication Center Activities

SCC–
Speech Communication Center

The SCC, located in MC 211, provides students with a flexible, self-paced, non-threatening learning environment to practice and review different aspects of effective public speaking. Our facility offers clients state of the art equipment, private and public practice areas, and a helpful friendly staff.

The SCC offers everyone the following opportunities:

- **Find out** your communication apprehension level by taking the Personal Report of Communication (PRCA).
- **Familiarize** yourself with speech assignment criteria by viewing other Del Mar students' recorded "A" speeches.
- **View** recorded speeches by well-known individuals of historical and/or political significance, all modeling effective presentational skills.
- **View** instructional materials which highlight areas of the public speaking process.
- **Learn** how to access appropriate research sources for your speeches.
- **Receive** help on outline formats and then type your speech preparation outline.
- **Create** computer generated visuals on PowerPoint for your upcoming classroom speeches. Practice incorporating them into your speech with our presentational equipment which is identical to the equipment utilized in the speech classrooms.
- **Practice** your speeches on camera. After recording your speech, watch and critique yourself. Receive feedback from a peer by having him/her complete the Partner Viewing Critique form found in this activity book.
- **Receive** one-on-one feedback about your communication skills from SCC consultants.
- **Participate** in scheduled workshops that will help, guide, and support you throughout the semester.

SCC hours may vary from semester to semester. Call 361-698-1581 for the schedule.

Recognizing PowerPoint DOs and DON'Ts

Objective

To learn and identify requirements for the creation of a PowerPoint slide show to be utilized as a visual aid for a speech presentation.

Instructions

[1] Your instructor will tell you how to access the PowerPoint DOs and DON'Ts slide shows.

[2] **Choose any three of the slide shows to view.** While/after viewing each slide show, answer the questions on the next page. You will be identifying the "DOs and DON'Ts" of using PowerPoint as a visual aid in a speech. (Each slide show will have more than three weaknesses and three strengths.) If you have difficulty identifying three of the requirements followed and three of the requirements violated, you should choose another slide show to view.

In order to correctly identify the requirements followed and violated, you will need to refer to the information covered in class for computer-generated visual aids and the "PowerPoint Requirements" provided on the page following this assignment. Understand that you will not receive credit if your responses to do not reference *specific* PowerPoint requirements.

Examples of DOs/DON'Ts that <u>WILL receive credit</u>:
"The font colors for titles and text are consistent throughout the slide show."
"There is correct grammar and spelling on all slides."
"The picture on slide #5 is too small to be seen by audience members in the back of the room."
"There is no blank slide at the end of the presentation."

Examples of DOs/DON'Ts that <u>WILL NOT receive credit</u>:
"Pretty picture."
"Just the right amount of slides."
"Crazy transitions."
"Too many words."

PowerPoint DOs (Strengths) and DON'Ts (Weaknesses)

• **Title of PowerPoint slide show:** _____

[1]   Identify three strengths. Be specific. Use PowerPoint requirements, or you will not receive credit.

_____

_____

_____

[2]   Identify three weaknesses. Be specific. Use PowerPoint requirements, or you will not receive credit.

_____

_____

_____

• **Title of PowerPoint slide show:** _____

[1]   Identify three strengths. Be specific. Use PowerPoint requirements, or you will not receive credit.

_____

_____

_____

[2]   Identify three weaknesses. Be specific. Use PowerPoint requirements, or you will not receive credit.

_____

_____

_____

• **Title of PowerPoint slide show:** _____

[1]   Identify three strengths. Be specific. Use PowerPoint requirements, or you will not receive credit.

_____

_____

_____

[2]   Identify three weaknesses. Be specific. Use PowerPoint requirements, or you will not receive credit.

_____

_____

_____

Basic PowerPoint Requirements

All students need to follow these guidelines when creating their slideshows:

Number of Slides

- Don't use your PowerPoint as your speech note cards.

- For a five to seven minute speech you should avoid an excessive amount of slides (i.e., 10+). Hit key points.

Blank/Title Slides

- Use a blank slide or a title slide at the beginning of your slideshow.
- If you use a title slide, it can have the title of your presentation on it but usually does not include your name, the date, and your class time.
- Insert a blank slide at the end of your slideshow. It should be the same background color that you have used throughout the slideshow.
- Utilize a blank screen whenever there is a time lapse between the information to be presented from one slide to the next.

Color

- Don't overuse. Be consistent with the same background color for each screen.
- When using a template (wallpaper background), make sure it is appropriate for the speech topic.
- Choose one color for titles and a separate color for text (unless instructed otherwise by your instructor).
- Maintain consistency in color of fonts.
- Choose a color for letters that contrasts with the slide's background (dark-colored letters on pale/light backgrounds and light-colored letters on dark backgrounds).

Fonts and Spacing

- Maintain consistency in choice of font (make sure it is not a font that is difficult to read/see).
- Size of font needs to be large enough for entire audience in the back of the room to see (minimum of 44–point for titles and 32–point for text).
- Boldface fonts if they are not already bold.
- Follow the "6–7 words/6–7 lines" rule to avoid a screen that is too busy or crowded.
- Maintain consistency in capitalization for titles and text.
- Use upper and lower case lettering (not all caps) for all titles and text.
- Maintain consistency in spacing.
- Frame/border your pictures/art when appropriate.
- Avoid too much blank space on slides.
- Align bullet points. Do not center them.
- Maintain even margins.
- Do not overlap letters and pictures. Words become difficult to read.

Wording

- Use phrases (not full sentences) for your text.
- Use parallel structure.
- Use correct grammar and spelling. Utilize the grammar and spelling checker.

Visual Images

- Use images related/appropriate to speech content.
- Use clip art, pictures, charts, etc. that are clear (not fuzzy) and large enough to be seen in the back of the classroom.
- Don't overuse visual images; avoid too many images on one slide. One good picture or drawing is usually sufficient. Two images/pictures are the limit on a single slide.
- Leave a margin around the edge of slides.
- Do not put text too close to pictures/images.
- Do not use cartoons or images that have a watermark stamp on them.
- Crop copyright information from pictures and images.

Animation and Sound

- Avoid distracting animation.
- Do not use sound unless you have incorporated streaming video.
- Adjust volume for streaming video so it is loud and clear.

Transitions and Custom Animation

- Use appropriate/non-distracting transitions and maintain consistency between every slide.
- Use "custom animation" when appropriate and be consistent in the form chosen (bring in one piece of bulleted information/full phrase at a time).

Name of Speaker _____

Name of Critiquer _____

Partner Viewing Critique

Objectives

To receive feedback on the effectiveness of your speech prior to presenting it in class for a grade and to use the critiquer's suggestions to improve content and/or delivery.

Instructions

Prior to the day of your speech delivery in the classroom, go to the SCC and record yourself practicing your speech. You should be standing up. Use your note cards and incorporate your visual aid. You may record your speech at home. Have another person view the recording and answer the questions on this critique about your speech content and delivery. Make sure he/she understands that all questions have to be responded to in a thorough and insightful manner.

[1] Did the speaker grab your attention at the very beginning of the speech? If so, why was the attention getting technique effective? Do you have any suggestions on how the speaker could improve the very start of the speech in terms of content and/or delivery?

_____

_____

_____

_____

[2] Describe how the speaker's voice either enhanced or detracted from the speech. What suggestions could you make to enhance vocal variety, articulation, pausing, rate of speaking, etc.? Be specific in your response.

_____

_____

_____

_____

[3] Describe the effectiveness of the speaker's nonverbal communication. Be specific when discussing eye contact or lack of it, body posture and movement, gestures, and facial expressions.

_____

_____

_____

_____

[4] What was the speaker's link to the topic? Did he/she clarify within the introduction why he/she chose to speak about this topic? Explain.

_____

_____

_____

_____

[5] Did the speaker link the topic to the audience (the intended audience being his/her speech class)? What was said in the introduction and/or throughout the speech that showed that audience analysis was done? Specifically, how did the speaker focus on why the audience should be interested in listening to the information provided by the speaker?

_____

_____

_____

_____

[6] Did the speaker end the speech effectively? Was it a strong ending? If not, do you have any suggestions on how the speaker could bring closure to the speech more effectively in regard to content and/or delivery?

_____

_____

_____

_____

Speech 1315

SCC ACTIVITY

Name of Speaker _____

Name of Critiquer _____

Partner Viewing Critique

Objectives

To receive feedback on the effectiveness of your speech prior to presenting it in class for a grade and to use the critiquer's suggestions to improve content and/or delivery.

Instructions

Prior to the day of your speech delivery in the classroom, go to the SCC and record yourself practicing your speech. You should be standing up. Use your note cards and incorporate your visual aid. You may record your speech at home. Have another person view the recording and answer the questions on this critique about your speech content and delivery. Make sure he/she understands that all questions have to be responded to in a thorough and insightful manner.

[1] Did the speaker grab your attention at the very beginning of the speech? If so, why was the attention getting technique effective? Do you have any suggestions on how the speaker could improve the very start of the speech in terms of content and/or delivery?

_____

_____

_____

_____

[2] Describe how the speaker's voice either enhanced or detracted from the speech. What suggestions could you make to enhance vocal variety, articulation, pausing, rate of speaking, etc.? Be specific in your response.

_____

_____

_____

_____

[3] Describe the effectiveness of the speaker's nonverbal communication. Be specific when discussing eye contact or lack of it, body posture and movement, gestures, and facial expressions.

_____

_____

_____

_____

[4] What was the speaker's link to the topic? Did he/she clarify within the introduction why he/she chose to speak about this topic? Explain.

_____

_____

_____

_____

[5] Did the speaker link the topic to the audience (the intended audience being his/her speech class)? What was said in the introduction and/or throughout the speech that showed that audience analysis was done? Specifically, how did the speaker focus on why the audience should be interested in listening to the information provided by the speaker?

_____

_____

_____

_____

[6] Did the speaker end the speech effectively? Was it a strong ending? If not, do you have any suggestions on how the speaker could bring closure to the speech more effectively in regard to content and/or delivery?

_____

_____

_____

_____

Expressive
Delivery:
Beak and Wings

BIRD SEED

Public Speaking Instructional DVD List

The following DVDs are available in the SCC, located in MC 211, and online on the SCC website. You will want to watch one or more of these DVDs to give you additional insights on particular communication issues.

DVDs cannot be checked out of the SCC, but you can watch them at your convenience during open SCC hours or anytime online.

The worksheets that follow will aid in your understanding and comprehension of the information in the specific DVDs addressed. The questions should be answered while viewing the DVD.

Speaking with Confidence: Ethics

Speaking with Confidence: Listening

Speaking with Confidence: Critiquing Public Speakers

Speaking with Confidence: The Audience

Speaking with Confidence: The Speaker

Speaking with Confidence: Selecting a Topic

Speaking with Confidence: Finding Information

Speaking with Confidence: Organization and Outlining

Speaking with Confidence: Introductions and Conclusions

Speaking with Confidence: Language

Speaking with Confidence: Delivery

Speaking with Confidence: Presentational Aids

Speaking with Confidence: Informative Speaking—Organization

Speaking with Confidence: Persuasive Speaking Strategies

Speaking with Confidence: Persuasive Speaking Organization

Name _____

Class Time _____

Speaking with Confidence: Ethics

[1] Communication is a powerful tool. Explain.

[2] What is the chief responsibility that comes with our right to free speech?

[3] List three moral ideals.

[4] Ethical speakers support their claims with _____ facts from _____ sources.

[5] Is it ethical to pass off hypothetical examples and situations as reality? Explain your answer.

[6] Define plagiarism.

[7] What is the ethical responsibility of listeners in an audience?

Speaking with Confidence: Listening

[1]   Explain the difference between hearing and listening.

[2]   Sign language is not only based on signing. What else is used to get the message across?

[3]   Active listening involves nonverbal communication. Explain which nonverbal features are indicative of active listening. What do nonverbal cues tell us?

[4]   Define *unconditional positive regard*.

[5]   Good listening skills are prerequisites in most careers. Dr. Lynne Holtz, family practice physician, looks for what specific listening skills?

[6]   Journalist Bill Kelly said that the less you know about a topic, the more you need to listen. List two reasons why we don't listen.

[7]   We need to listen to what people _____ as well as what people _____.

Speaking with Confidence: Critiquing Public Speakers

[1]   Rank the three sample excerpts at the beginning of the tape (with #1 being the one you liked the best) and explain why you ranked the speakers in this order.

[2]   What should fair evaluators avoid when critiquing a speaker? What are the results of Judy Pearson's research concerning gender differences in speech evaluation procedures?

[3]   List four things on which an evaluator should focus.

[4]   In your opinion, explain which is more important—the delivery or the content of the speech. Be specific in your response.

[5]   What was the message (regarding the critique) of each student interviewed?

[6]   The video stresses the importance of critiquing the speech, not the person. Why is it better to give constructive criticism in a written format?

[7]   List four of the tips suggested for giving constructive criticism.

Name _____

Class Time _____

Speaking with Confidence: The Audience

[1]   What should be a speaker's primary focus?

[2]   In your own words, what is audience analysis?

[3]   What are demographics? What are some examples of demographics?

[4]   What are psychographics?

[5]   How would you gather information about demographics or psychographics?

[6]   If you do not have ready access to your audience, what is the best way to learn about them?

[7]   How did the three speakers change their topics in order to adapt to their audience? Be specific.

Speaking with Confidence: The Speaker

[1]   What distinguishes a reliable source from an unreliable one?

[2]   Explain why establishing credibility as a speaker is important.

[3]   What influence does appearance and language have on a speaker's credibility?

[4]   List the four dimensions of source credibility.

[5]   Does the same consideration of source credibility apply to debate and public speaking?

[6]   Briefly explain how a speaker can emphasize characteristic commonalities without sounding "fake."

[7]   What is the most important thing to remember about audience trust?

Speaking with Confidence: Selecting a Topic

[1] According to Gustav W. Friedrich, what are some ways to find topics for your speeches?

[2] What are two lists you should make before writing your speech?

[3] On what does your success depend when speaking?

[4] What are the six guidelines to follow when selecting your speech topic? Clarify why each is important.

[5] What are the four ways to determine if your topic is appropriate?

[6] According to Sharon Ratliffe, what should your purpose be when choosing your topic?

[7] What speech topics should be avoided?

Speaking with Confidence: Finding Information

[1] Hubert Brown and Paul Nelson, the narrators of this video, discuss how a speaker can use him/
herself as a source of information in speeches. After listening to the two speech excerpts, share how
the speakers drew on their personal experience in each of their speeches.

[2] Utilizing information gained from "experts" is also suggested as a source for speeches. How do
you know whom to contact to get specific information? Share some of the suggestions Hubert
Brown discusses.

[3] While there is a great deal of information available electronically, and there are definite advantages to
"libraries without walls," it is also noted that electronic information is not necessarily better in all cases.
State two reasons given why print sources available in libraries may be the best sources of information
for some speech topics.

[4] According to Paul Nelson, one of the video narrators, how many sources do you need for an
effective speech?

[5] How can a reference librarian specifically help you with your speech?

[6] What is an oral footnote? How should you credit your sources in a speech? What information needs to be included?

[7] The three reasons why individuals should not plagiarize are: it is unethical, rhetorically "dumb," and there can be dire consequences. Share the example Paul Nelson refers to with respect to a dean's plagiarism and the consequences that occurred.

Speaking with Confidence: Organization and Outlining

[1]   Why is it important to have organization in your speech? Why is outlining an essential step in the speech making process?

[2]   What are the seven patterns of speech organization?

[3]   What are the three main points involved in outlining?

[4]   What are the five parts to Monroe's Motivated Sequence? What is the most ignored part of this organizational format?

[5]   Explain the difference between anti-climactic and climactic. How can this be used in a speech?

[6]   Can only one pattern per speech be used? Explain your answer.

[7]   How many points per speech are acceptable? What percentage of a speech should this cover?

Speaking with Confidence: Introductions and Conclusions

[1]   What are the four functions of the introduction, according to the moderators of the video, Hubert Brown and Judy Pearson?

[2]   The moderators share two examples from their speaking experience about how they gained attention in two of their speeches. What were the examples they shared?

[3]   Why is audience analysis so important in the introduction of your speech?

[4]   What is the purpose of the preview in an introduction?

[5]   According to the video, what are the three functions of the speech conclusion?

[6]   According to the video, a conclusion should be short but _____. Give two examples of concluding techniques from the video (either from the speech examples or the comedian's life experience).

[7]   According to the moderators of the video, Hubert Brown and Judy Pearson, what is the goal of your speech?

Name _____

Class Time _____

Speaking with Confidence: Language

[1] What limits our language choices?

[2] No matter what personal, political, or social climate your speech is delivered in, what do you need to consider?

[3] On what are the differences in language based?

[4] Define "oral language."

[5] What is your purpose as a communicator?

[6] What occurs when you take complex issues and reduce them to sound-byte size?

[7] What is the term used that signifies making a distinction and implying a judgment?

Name _____

Class Time _____

Speaking with Confidence: Delivery

[1]   What is the most important factor affecting your delivery?

[2]   What should you consider when selecting a mode of presentation? Identify two factors.

[3]   Explain the advantages and disadvantages of each mode of delivery.

Manuscript   *Advantage:*
                    Disadvantage:

Memorization   *Advantage:*
                    Disadvantage:

Impromptu   *Advantage:*
                    Disadvantage:

Extemporaneous   *Advantage:*
                    Disadvantage:

[4]   When you use the memorization mode of delivery, what three things do you need to memorize?

[5]   Which mode of delivery is considered the worst for a student to use?

[6]   Which mode of delivery is most requested for business presentations?

[7]   What are the three vocal aspects of delivery?

Name _____

Class Time _____

Speaking with Confidence: Presentational Aids

[1] What is the main purpose of visual aids?

[2] List the six factors to consider when contemplating whether or not to use presentational aids.

[3] When are presentational aids inappropriate?

[4] Explain the "Three Bs."

[5] What four standards should be considered when selecting visual aids?

[6] Explain the "Five Ps" of planning.

[7] What are five ways that visual aids add to a presentation?

Speaking with Confidence: Informative Speaking Organization

[1] What is the main goal for an informative speech?

[2] What are the three parts of a speech?

[3] Identify two important things to consider when selecting a speech topic.

[4] What are the three things you should do in your introduction?

[5] What are the four organizational patterns that you can use in the body of your speech? Give an example for each organizational pattern.

[6] What should be included in your speech conclusion?

[7] What are the four types of informative speeches?

Name _____

Class Time _____

Speaking with Confidence: Persuasive Speaking Strategies

[1] Persuasive speaking tries to influence change in the audience's _____ and
_____ concerning the topic.

[2] History tells us that persuasive speakers have succeeded sometimes and other times failed to change
_____.

[3] List and define the two types of proofs Aristotle identified.

[4] Define logos, pathos, ethos, and mythos.

[5] What do persuasive speakers attempt to shape, reinforce, and/or change?

[6] What are the principles of persuasion?

Name _____

Class Time _____

Speaking with Confidence: Persuasive Speaking Organization

[1]   What are the three general reasons why we make persuasive speeches?

[2]   Define an "argument" as discussed in this recording.

[3]   Define "evidence." Give some examples.

[4]   People are motivated by logic as well as _____.

[5]   What are examples of negative emotional arguments?

[6]   What are the "bricks" of your persuasive speech?

[7]   What are the five parts/steps in Monroe's Motivated Sequence?

Written Activities

Analyzing Your Audience

Before you develop your speech, you need to spend some time constructing an audience profile. You will begin to learn about your public speaking classmates on an informal level as the semester progresses. You will be picking up information about them from comments made, questions asked, and topics chosen for speeches. You also have the unique ability to analyze your audience on a more formal level through oral questioning and written survey questionnaires.

The information you gather will help you to discover what prior knowledge or familiarity your audience has about your specific topic. This will help you tailor your message to this specific audience. You will also use this information to clarify in your speech introduction how your speech topic is relevant to the audience. Thoughtful audience analysis will answer the question that most audience members are thinking, "What's in this for me?" The two ways to analyze your audience using a question format are as follows:

[1] **Orally** asking fixed-alternative questions, which your audience members can easily respond to by a raise of hands, is often called informal audience analysis. (i.e., "How many of you have ever been hospitalized for any kind of surgery or injury?" or "How many of you eat out at a fast food restaurant at least once a week?" Remember to only ask questions that your audience members would not feel threatened or embarrassed to respond to in a group environment.

[2] **Written questionnaires,** which survey your audience, are a method of formal audience analysis. (i.e., "Have you ever contemplated suicide?" or "Have you ever been physically abused in a relationship?") Audience members will be more likely to respond honestly if these types of questions are distributed in a written format and can be responded to anonymously.

If you're speaking to an audience with whom you are totally unfamiliar, some audience analysis information can be gained from the individual who asked you to speak. This contact person can identify specific audience members who may be attending your speech, and you can contact them individually for a brief interview.

Types of Audience Analysis Survey Questions

Yes/No Questions: **Do you know your cholesterol level?** ___Yes ___No

Scale Questions: **Put an X on the scale to show your answer.**
I believe that a large portion of state lottery revenue should go to support Texas public education.

Strongly Agree   Agree   Not Sure   Disagree   Strongly Disagree

←——→

Checklist: **In which of the following situations have you found yourself?**
__ Overdrew checking account, checks bounced
__ Overdrew debit account
__ Made only minimum payments on credit cards
__ Received late notices or calls from creditors
__ Merchandise repossessed due to non-payment
__ Denied loan due to credit rating
__ None of the preceding situations has ever happened to me.

Multiple Choice: **The number of persons in Nueces County who have diabetes is:**
a.   400
b.   4,000
c.   40,000
d.   100,000

Ranking: **Where do you eat your meals? Rank from 1 (most often) to 4 (least often).**
___ Home ___ Restaurant ___Vending Machines ___ Fast Food Places

Open Ended Questions: **Name three fears or concerns you have about donating blood.**

Name _____

Class Time _____

Instructions for the Informative Audience Analysis Survey

Instructions

Create an Informative Speech Audience Analysis Survey meeting the following requirements:

- **CREATE FIVE QUESTIONS: using (at least) <u>three different question formats</u>.**
- **DO NOT put your name on the survey.**
- **Put a piece of clip art on the survey.**
- **Put Male/Female at the top of the survey.**

IMPORTANT:

- Remember your survey questions should help you link your audience to your informative speech topic. **Do not include more than one question that attempts to find out what your audience knows or doesn't know about your topic.** The response/s you receive to that question only validates that you are going to be delivering an informative speech (telling us something that we don't know).

- **Write the other four questions so that the responses give you a way to link your audience to the specific topic or to the topic in general.** For example: If you were going to deliver your informative speech on tarantulas, you could ask "Are you afraid of bugs and/or spiders?"

  yes___; no___ or "Rank your fear of bugs and/or spiders."

  1 (no fear) __; 2 (little fearful) __; 3 (afraid) __ ; 4 (very afraid) __; 5 (extremely afraid)__

  In this case, the responses will probably help link the audience to bugs/spiders in general. It wouldn't be necessary to link your audience specifically to tarantulas.

- **Bring ____ copies of the survey to class on the due date—enough copies for all of your classmates.** You may want to create your survey on the top half of the page and then cut and paste it to the bottom half of the page. Since you can then cut your pages in half, you will not have to print as many copies of the survey.

  The information you gain from your Informative Speech Audience Analysis Survey will help you complete the Audience Analysis Survey Summary found in this activity book. All of this work is in preparation for the writing of your informative speech. Linking your audience to your speech topic is included in your speech introduction.

Survey Examples for the Informative Speech

MALE/FEMALE

[1]   Do you know how fast you usually drive?

      Yes   No   Not Sure

[2]   What is the speed limit in school zones?

      5 MPH   10 MPH   15 MPH   20 MPH

[3]   Do you use a blinker to change lanes while you are driving?

      Yes   No   Sometimes

[4]   What do you think would motivate people to drive safely?

[5]   I follow the speed limit all of the time.

      Strongly Agree   Agree   Not Sure   Disagree

MALE/FEMALE

[1]   Do you like sailboats?

      Yes   No   Not Sure

[2]   How many times have you been sailing?

      Never   1–2   3–4   5 or more

[3]   I feel comfortable on the water.

      Strongly Agree   Agree   Not Sure   Disagree   Strongly Disagree

[4]   I have heard about the Corpus Christi Marina's Sailboat Races.

      Yes   No

[5]   Mark below if any apply to you.

    ☐ Haven't been sailing because it scares me.

    ☐ I don't know anyone who sails or has a sail boat.

    ☐ I can't swim.

    ☐ Seems like an expensive activity.

Name _____

Class Time _____

Informative Audience Analysis Survey Summary

Instructions

- Compile the results of your survey responses on a blank survey [i.e., how many said yes, how many said no; how many answered (a), how many answered (b), etc.].
- Answer questions 1 and 2 below.
- Staple this Survey Summary to a copy of your survey with the compiled responses and turn in both to your instructor.

[1] What are you going to say in your speech introduction to link yourself to your speech topic? In other words, why did you choose your topic?

[2] What are you going to say in your speech introduction to link your audience to your speech topic using the information gained from the responses from your audience analysis survey? DO NOT SHARE WHAT THE AUDIENCE KNOWS OR DOESN'T KNOW ABOUT THE TOPIC—THAT IS NOT A LINK! THAT JUST CLARIFIES THAT YOU ARE GIVING AN INFORMATIVE SPEECH. The question "What's in this speech for me?" is on your audience's minds. Tell them! That's how you link your audience to your topic.

Instructions for the Persuasive Audience Analysis Survey

Instructions

Create a Persuasive Speech Audience Analysis Survey meeting the following requirements:

- **3–5 questions:** You can use any question format you choose for the first 1–4 questions (multiple choice, yes/no, scale, etc.) **except for an open-ended question.**
- **The LAST QUESTION needs to include the following open-ended question: "Why do you think some people may be hesitant to contribute to _____ (fill in your organization's name)?"** It is considered to be an open-ended question because everyone will have to fill in their responses.
- **Do NOT put your name on the survey.**
- **Put the non-profit organization name at the top of the survey.**
- **Put a piece of clip art on the survey.**
- **Put Male/Female at the top of the survey.**

IMPORTANT

- **Questions on your survey should be an attempt to link your audience to the problem/issues that your organization addresses.** For example, if your organization's main mission is to help the homeless, ask questions that will link your audience to the homeless and identify why your listeners should care about the problems/issues the homeless face. (Do they know someone who is/was homeless? Are they aware—from what they see on our streets—that we have a large homeless population? If your listeners don't have savings to fall back on, and the circumstances in their changed drastically, is it in the realm of possibility that they could be homeless at some point?)

- **Bring _____ copies of your survey to class on the due date—enough for all of your classmates.** You may want to create your survey on the top half of the page and then cut and paste it to the bottom half of the page. Since you can then cut your pages in half, you will not have to print as many copies of the survey.

The responses you gain from your Persuasive Speech Audience Analysis Survey will help you complete the Persuasive Speech Audience Analysis Survey Summary found in this activity book. All of this work is in preparation for the writing of your persuasive speech. Linking your audience to your speech topic is included in your speech introduction.

Survey Examples for the Persuasive Speech

Dress for Success

MALE/FEMALE

[1] In the past year, how many times have you donated clothes to charity?

   Never   1–2 times   3–4 times   5–6 times   7 or more times

[2] Are you, or any female you know, in need of a job?

   Yes   No

[3] What someone wears (clothing, shoes, etc) to an interview has a big impact on the impression made and how successful he/she is at getting the job.

   Strongly Agree   Agree   Not Sure   Disagree   Strongly Disagree

[4] Why do you think that some people might be hesitant to contribute money to the Dress for Success Organization?

Coastal Bend Wellness Foundation

MALE/FEMALE

[1] Have you ever known anyone who has been affected by HIV/AIDS?

   Yes   No

[2] How many people do you think have been affected by HIV/AIDS in Nueces County over the past year?

   10–20   20–30   30–40   50–70   Over 70

[3] Persons in these jobs are at risk for contacting HIV through occupational exposure. (circle one or more)

   Groundskeepers   Dentists

   Police Officers   Healthcare Workers

   Firefighters   Custodians

   Laboratory workers   Rescue workers

[4] Why do you think that some people might be hesitant to contribute money to the Coastal Bend Wellness Foundation?

Name _____

Class Time _____

Persuasive Audience Analysis Survey Summary

(For a persuasive speech in support of a non-profit organization)

Instructions

- **Compile the results of your survey responses on a blank survey [i.e., how many said yes, how many said no; how many answered (a), how many answered (b), etc.].**
- **Answer questions 1 and 2 below.**
- **Staple this Survey Summary to a copy of your survey with the compiled responses and turn in both to your instructor.**

[1] What are you going to say in your speech introduction to link yourself to your speech topic? In other words, why did you choose your topic? This may be a link to the organization or to the problem(s) the organization addresses.

[2] What are you going to say in your speech introduction to link your audience to your speech topic using the information gained from the responses from your audience analysis survey? Link your listeners to the problem(s) that the organization addresses. In other words, answer the questions that the audience is asking, "What's in this speech for me? Why should I care?" (At this point, do NOT share if your audience doesn't know anything about your organization or the problem(s) it addresses because that is NOT an audience link. Neither are the survey responses about why someone might be hesitant to support this organization an audience link.)

Name _____

Class Time _____

Audience Analysis: Demographic Information

Check what applies to you (adding an additional category if you choose to do so).

Age Range
____under 18
____18–24
____25–35
____36 and over

Gender:
____male
____female

Marital Status:
____single
____married
____engaged
____domestic partnership
____divorced
____widowed

Children:
____no children
____one child
____more than one

Religious Preference:
____Catholic
____Christian (non Catholic)
____Jewish
____Muslim
____agnostic
____Jehovah Witness
____atheist
____other

Political Affiliation:
____Democrat
____Republican
____Independent
____non-political
____other

Employment Status:
____unemployed
____work part-time
____work full-time

Jobs Held:
____sales
____medical
____restaurant
____office
____fast food
____education
____self-employed
____construction
____other

Life Style: Majority of time spent in:
____city (size of Corpus Christi)
____metropolitan area (Larger city—size of Houston)
____rural area

Time spent in South Texas area:
____0–2 years
____3–5 years
____over 5 years

College Major:
____undecided
____education
____arts
____medical
____business
____law/criminal justice
____communication
____other

Name _____

Class Time _____

"Great Speeches" Critique

Objective

Great speeches are deemed "great" because they illustrate certain characteristics of effective rhetorical communication. Although these speeches are recognized for their excellence by communications experts, they are most often remembered for their appeal to the general public. This assignment will give you the opportunity to see significant speeches by national leaders and to evaluate the impact of their verbal and nonverbal messages.

Instructions

- Speeches by well known individuals are available for viewing both online and in the SCC. Your instructor will provide you with a list. Select only one speaker for this assignment.
- Listen to an ENTIRE speech before beginning your evaluation.
- After viewing one "great" speech, answer the following questions on a separate sheet. Include the name of the speaker and the name of his/her speech. Be sure to answer all questions THOROUGHLY in complete sentences. Be very specific. Use exact quotations and ideas from the speech whenever applicable. Attach this critique form to your responses.

[1] What national and/or international events were occurring that prompted the giving of this speech? Be specific. (10 points)

[2] What was the intention of the speaker? What did he/she hope to accomplish with this speech? (10 points)

[3] In your opinion, what was the probable (or actual) effect on the audience to whom this speech was delivered? On what do you base your comments? Be specific. (10 points)

[4] Determine why, with your present understanding of rhetorical communication, this speech is a "great" speech. Discuss at least three reasons. Put some thought into your reasons. (15 points)

[5] a. How did the speaker grab the attention of the audience? What did he/she say? Was the attention getter effective? Why or why not? (10 points)

b. What were the main points of the speech? Use quotations from the speech. (10 points)

c. How did the speaker conclude the speech? Be specific. (10 points)

[6]   Describe the non-verbal communication of the speaker: (a) eye contact, (b) gestures, (c) facial expression. Was it appropriate? Why or why not? Be specific. (15 points)

[7]   Describe how the speaker's voice either enhanced or detracted from the speech. Be specific. (10 points)

* *Staple* this signed worksheet to your paper before you turn in your responses.

Speech 1315   Name _____

WRITTEN ACTIVITY   Class Time _____

Speech Showcase Critique

Objective

Since 1987, the Communications Department of Del Mar College has sponsored a "Speech Showcase" at the end of every semester. The purpose of the Showcase is to highlight good speakers from our classes. The speeches selected for the Showcase are speeches originally given in the classroom setting and repeated for the Showcase audience. Viewing Showcase speeches will allow you to see excellent examples of student presentations. Preparing a critique on a speech will reinforce your ability to recognize appropriate delivery skills, organizational skills, and speech content.

Instructions

Select for viewing ONE Showcase speech. These speeches are available for viewing on the SCC website. On a separate sheet, thoroughly answer the following ten questions in complete sentences.

Attach this critique form to your responses.

[1]   Describe the clothing worn by the speaker. Was it appropriate? Why or why not? (10 points)

[2]   Were audio/visual aids used effectively? Discuss the aid or aids used. Did the speaker and his/her aid comply with our class discussion about the proper use of audio/visuals? Be specific. Give at least one example of how it did or did not follow class guidelines. (10 points)

[3]   List the references the speaker cited. Were they credible? Why or why not? Be specific. (10 points)

[4]   How could you tell if audience analysis had or had not been done? How did the speaker appeal to the local (Corpus Christi) audience? (10 points)

[5]   How did the speaker give the audience an incentive to listen? Did he/she show common ground? (10 points)

[6]   What was the speaker's link to his/her subject? (10 points)

[7]   What organizational pattern did the speaker use? (10 points)

[8]   List three different kinds of support materials the speaker used. (Support materials include: statistics, testimony, examples, narratives, definitions, etc.) Give an example from the speech of each one you selected. (10 points)

[9]   Look for all functions in the conclusion of the speech. Identify each of them within the conclusion by writing down the actual words of the speaker. If any function is missing, identify it. (10 points)

[10] If you could give the speaker advice about improving his/her speech, what would it be? Give advice on the speech itself and on its delivery. (10 points)

Staple this signed worksheet to your responses.

Name _____

Class Time _____

Professional Speaker Critique

Objectives

To sharpen your skills as a critical listener outside of the classroom environment and to give you practice as a speech evaluator.

Instructions

[1]   Attend a speech by someone who makes his or her living from an occupation which involves public speaking. Possible speakers may include political candidates, educators, ministers, television personalities, salespersons, newscasters, and those persons considered "experts" in their fields. The speech must be a prepared speech with an introduction, body, and conclusion. (A press conference, award acceptance speech, etc. DOES NOT fit this description.)

[2]   Be a critical and analytical listener as you observe the presentation. Use the questions on the back of this sheet to critique the speaker's content, organization, and delivery.

[3]   Your answers should be written in full sentences, stapled to this signed worksheet, and turned in to your instructor.

[4]   Don't hesitate to be honest in your appraisal of the speaker. Be clear and specific about his/her weaknesses and/or strengths as a public speaker.

Professional Speaker Critique Questions

[1] Who is the speaker you observed? What is his/her occupation? Did the speaker clarify the purpose of the presentation and why he/she is a credible speaker on the topic? Discuss thoroughly. (10 points)

[2] At what location was the speech delivered? What was the reason or occasion for this speech? (10 points)

[3] Did the speaker show any visible signs of speech anxiety? If so, clarify what they were. If not, what methods do you think were used to help "cover up" any signs of anxiety that may have been present? Give specific examples. (10 points)

[4] Did the speaker use notes? If so, what kind? Did he/she seem well prepared? How did you come to this conclusion? Be specific. (10 points)

[5] Was the speaker's introduction effective? If not, how could the introduction be improved? What "grabber" was used to get the audience's interest? Did the speaker relate his/her topic to this particular audience by establishing common ground? How could you tell? Be specific in your responses. (10 points)

[6] What type of supporting materials (testimony, statistics, narratives, examples, definitions, analogies, etc.) did the speaker use to develop his/her topic? Were they interesting and/or convincing? Give an example. (10 points)

[7] Was the speaker's conclusion effective? If not, how could it be improved? What was the speaker's "clincher"? (10 points)

[8] Discuss the audience's verbal/nonverbal reaction to the speaker. Be specific in your responses by detailing actual audience responses. (10 points)

[9] Discuss how the speaker's delivery was effective or ineffective. Address all of the following areas: eye contact, gestures, movement, posture, vocal variety, word choice, sincerity, and enthusiasm. (10 points)

[10] Did you like or dislike the speaker's overall performance? Why? What specifically could the speaker have done differently to improve his/her presentation? (10 points)

Name _____

Class Time _____

Critiquing a Feature Film

Purpose

The art of *criticism* allows a person to evaluate and analyze someone else's work. Movies, art shows, plays, dance performances, speeches, and other presentations often invite critics to evaluate both the positive and negative aspects of the performance.

In order to be an effective critic, you must be a critical listener and viewer. Because movies are primarily an entertainment medium, viewing them for analysis—in this case communication analysis—requires forethought and direction. The goal of this assignment is to offer a measure of both.

Characteristics of good critiquing include:

[1] It is objective.

[2] It is definite. Avoid generalized comments such as "I'm not sure, but ..." or "It sort of ..."

[3] It is understandable and organized.

[4] It contains praise as well as suggestions for improvement.

[5] It avoids ridicule and sarcasm.

Instructions

Watch a full-length feature film of your choosing. Many titles are available for viewing in the SCC, or you may watch a movie at home or online. Guidelines that are to be followed are: 1. The movie is in English with no subtitles; 2. The movie has significant dialogue; 3. The movie's content allows you to answer the questions below.

For this assignment, please answer the following questions. *Answer in complete sentences in a thorough and insightful manner.* In **each** answer, use direct examples from dialogue, characters, and scenes from the movie.

[1] Who is the target audience for this film? Does the movie "reach" the intended target audience? Was audience analysis done? (10 pts.)

[2] Select a significant character and analyze his/her listening abilities. Discuss a specific scene (complete with dialogue) that illustrates the character's listening style. (10 pts.)

[3] Discuss an incident when a character shows communication anxiety. (10 pts.)

[4] Discuss a scene where a character shows/does not show ethical communication. (10 pts.)

[5] Analyze the way this feature film presented information that the audience needed to know. Find examples of four of these: narrative, statistics, literal analogy, figurative analogy, definition, quotations, hypothetical example, real example, contrast, testimony. You may use any of these more than once. (20 pts.)

[6] Discuss at least three reasons why you would/would not recommend this movie to a friend. You may address any aspect of the movie including direction, plot, characters, acting, costuming, etc. (15 pts.)

Please staple this assignment to your answers.

Name _____

Class Time _____

Use of Persuasion in the Media

Objective

Since we are surrounded by media forces sending us persuasive messages, it is important for us to be critical thinkers as we receive these messages. This assignment will help you to identify elements of persuasion and identify and evaluate persuasion in a real-world context.

Instructions

Choose *two* of these six infomercial clips that can be found on YouTube. (Your instructor might give you alternative choices to view.)

<u>YouTube</u>

Proactive X out Acne Cream 2013

Berman on the Magic Bullet Infomercial

Tony Little and WWF's The Genius Infomercial

Worx-GT 2-in-1 Trimmer/Edger

ShamWow (Full length)

My Lil Reminder (120 second TV spot))

Next, identify the following for each of the infomercial clips that you watched.

I. Rational Arguments/Evidence

    A.   What type of evidence do they give?

    B.   What type of statistics do they give and are they relevant and credible?

    C.   Is testimony (peer and expert) used? Explain.

    D.   Do they compare their product to other options? Which ones?

II. Emotional/Motivational Appeals

    A.   Do they use fear appeals? (i.e. "What would you do if you lost your job?")

    B.   Do they appeal to basic needs and values? (i.e. "Don't you want to be healthy and live a long life?")

    C.   Do they appeal to our self-interest? (i.e. "With these tapes, you will be rich and famous.")

    D.   Do they use a social proof? (i.e. "Everybody is doing it " or "This is a best selling product.")

E. Does the infomercial convey warmth? (i.e. Is there an emotional heart wrenching story or does it evoke an "awwh" when watching?)

III. Credibility

A. How is the presenter's expertise and authority built?

B. Does the presenter build good will and if so, how? (i.e. "We want to help you lose weight.")

C. Describe the salesperson and his or her personality as demonstrated in the infomercial, clarifying any "charisma" that is conveyed.

IV. Aesthetic Strategies

A. How is the visual presentation persuasive? (i.e. the setting or the backdrop)

B. Does music play a persuasive role? (i.e. Is the background music fast or slow and does it facilitate persuasion?)

C. What role does nonverbal communication play? (i.e. How are the presenters depicted nonverbally? Use of gesturing?)

V. Audience (Who is the intended audience and how do you know who they are?)

VI. Fallacies in Reasoning: (Does the infomercial demonstrate any fallacies in reasoning that are discussed in your textbook or that we discussed in class?)

VII. Organizational Format: Explain how the infomercial follows Monroe's Motivated Sequence

A. ATTENTION

B. NEED

C. SATISFACTION

D. VISUALIZATION

E. ACTION

Speech 1315

WRITTEN ACTIVITY

Name ______________________________

Class Time ______________________________

Self-Viewing Feedback Guide

Type of Speech: ______________________________

Instructor: ______________________________

Turn in this signed, completed form to your instructor on the date assigned. Be insightful and thorough.

[A] Immediately after giving your speech, answer the following questions. Be thorough!

[1] Rate your performance from 1 (lowest) to 10 (highest). Explain your answer. Be specific.

[2] What was the most effective element of your presentation? Be very specific.

[3] What would you do differently if you could do the speech again?

[B] After viewing your speech and reading the critiques from your peers and your instructor, answer the questions on the back of this page.

[1] What **pleased** you the most about your speech content and/or delivery?

[2] What **surprised** you the most about your speech content and/or delivery?

[3] Considering the feedback you've been given from your peers and your instructor, and your impressions while watching your recorded speech, list at least two ways you could improve your performance.

[4] Discuss what you have learned from this speaking assignment.

Speech 1315 Name ______________________

WRITTEN ACTIVITY Class Time ______________________

Self-Viewing Feedback Guide

Type of Speech: ______________________

Instructor: ______________________

Turn in this signed, completed form to your instructor on the date assigned. Be insightful and thorough.

[A] Immediately after giving your speech, answer the following questions. Be thorough!

[1] Rate your performance from 1 (lowest) to 10 (highest). Explain your answer. Be specific.

[2] What was the most effective element of your presentation? Be very specific.

[3] What would you do differently if you could do the speech again?

[B] After viewing your speech and reading the critiques from your peers and your instructor, answer the questions on the back of this page.

[1] What **<u>pleased</u>** you the most about your speech content and/or delivery?

[2] What **<u>surprised</u>** you the most about your speech content and/or delivery?

[3] Considering the feedback you've been given from your peers and your instructor, and your impressions while watching your recorded speech, list at least two ways you could improve your performance.

[4] Discuss what you have learned from this speaking assignment.

Speech 1315 Name ______________________

WRITTEN ACTIVITY Class Time ______________________

Self-Viewing Feedback Guide

Type of Speech: ______________________

Instructor: ______________________

Turn in this signed, completed form to your instructor on the date assigned. Be insightful and thorough.

[A] Immediately after giving your speech, answer the following questions. Be thorough!

[1] Rate your performance from 1 (lowest) to 10 (highest). Explain your answer. Be specific.

[2] What was the most effective element of your presentation? Be very specific.

[3] What would you do differently if you could do the speech again?

[B] After viewing your speech and reading the critiques from your peers and your instructor, answer the questions on the back of this page.

[1]   What **pleased** you the most about your speech content and/or delivery?

[2]   What **surprised** you the most about your speech content and/or delivery?

[3]   Considering the feedback you've been given from your peers and your instructor, and your impressions while watching your recorded speech, list at least two ways you could improve your performance.

[4]   Discuss what you have learned from this speaking assignment.

Group Activities

Name _____

Class Time _____

Audience Analysis, Specific Purpose, and Central Idea Practice

Instructions

In the following activity, you are to complete the areas that are left blank. You are provided the speech topics and the general purposes for possible informative speeches. In all instances, you will need to write two audience analysis questions that will aid the speaker to link the topic to the audience. In some instances, you will need to write a specific purpose statement and the central idea. Make sure that you follow the guidelines for all three of these tasks.

[1] **SPEECH TOPIC:** Credit Card Nightmares

    AUDIENCE ANALYSIS QUESTIONS: (Two questions that you could ask the audience to determine their link to the topic and to discover how informed they are about the topic.)

    GENERAL PURPOSE: To inform

    SPECIFIC PURPOSE: At the end of my speech, the audience will be able to explain how to avoid credit card theft.

    CENTRAL IDEA:

[2] **SPEECH TOPIC:** Scoliosis

    AUDIENCE ANALYSIS QUESTIONS: (Two questions you could ask the audience to determine their link to the topic and to discover how informed they are about the topic.)

    GENERAL PURPOSE: To inform

    SPECIFIC PURPOSE:

    CENTRAL IDEA: Scoliosis, which is a curvature of the spine, can be treated by physical therapy, a body brace, and surgery.

[3]   **SPEECH TOPIC:** Massage Therapy

AUDIENCE ANALYSIS QUESTIONS: (Two questions you could ask the audience to determine their link to the topic and to discover how much they know about the topic.)

GENERAL PURPOSE: To inform

SPECIFIC PURPOSE:

CENTRAL IDEA: Three major forms of massage therapy are Swedish massage, Trigger Point massage, and reflexology.

[4]   **SPEECH TOPIC:** Food-Borne Illnesses

AUDIENCE ANALYSIS: (Two questions you could ask the audience to determine their link to the topic and to discover how much they know about the topic.)

GENERAL PURPOSE: To inform

SPECIFIC PURPOSE: At the end of my speech, the audience will be able to explain how to prevent food-borne illnesses.

CENTRAL IDEA:

[5] **SPEECH TOPIC:** The Elements of Hip Hop Culture

AUDIENCE ANALYSIS QUESTIONS: (Two questions you could ask the audience to determine their link to the topic and to discover how informed they are about the topic.)

GENERAL PURPOSE: To inform

SPECIFIC PURPOSE:

CENTRAL IDEA: The four distinct elements that characterize Hip Hop are rap music (oral), DJing (aural), break dancing (physical), and graffiti art (visual).

[6] **SPEECH TOPIC:** Going on a Cruise as a Popular Vacation

AUDIENCE ANALYSIS QUESTIONS: (Two questions you could ask the audience to determine their link to the topic and discover how informed they are about the topic.)

GENERAL PURPOSE: To inform

SPECIFIC PURPOSE: At the end of my speech the audience will be able to explain why cruising has become a popular vacation option for travelers.

CENTRAL IDEA:

Scrambled Recipes—An Exercise on Topic, Purpose, and Central Idea

Part One

Preparing a complete "recipe" for a good speech involves creating a clear topic, general purpose, specific purpose, and central idea. Like any recipe, the "ingredients" must be written in the correct form, and the steps must be followed in the correct order. See if you can unscramble these speech "recipes."

[1] Topic _____

A. Surfing

[2] General Purpose_____

B. The modern sport of surfing gained popularity in the 1960s, but its history goes back to Polynesia in 1500 BC.

[3] Specific Purpose_____

C. To inform

[4] Central Idea_____

D. At the end of my speech, the audience will be able to explain the history of surfing.

---

[5] Topic_____

A. At the end of my speech, the audience will stop eating fast foods.

[6] General Purpose_____

B. Drive By, Not Through McDonald's

[7] Specific Purpose_____

C. To persuade

[8] Central Idea_____

D. Fast food chains usually offer non-nutritious foods that are high in fat, cholesterol, and calories.

---

[9] Topic_____

A. To inform

[10] General Purpose_____

B. Gamblers Anonymous is a 12-step program that addresses the recovery of compulsive gamblers.

[11] Specific Purpose_____

C. At the end of my speech, the audience will be able to explain how gamblers receive help through Gamblers Anonymous.

[12] Central Idea_____

D. Gamblers Anonymous

Part Two

In the following "recipes," one ingredient is missing. You need to add it, but be sure it complements the other ingredients.

[1] **Topic** • Don't Take Me Out to the Ball Game

    General Purpose • To persuade

    Specific Purpose • At the end of my speech, the audience will agree that baseball has lost its position as America's favorite pastime.

    Central Idea •

[2] **Topic** • Federal Assault Weapons Ban

    General Purpose • To persuade

    Specific Purpose •

    Central Idea • The Federal Assault Weapons Ban, which prohibited the manufacture for civilian use of semi-automatic firearms, became defunct in 2004, but it should be renewed.

Part Three

Now that you are an experienced chef, it's time to create your own recipes.

[1] **Topic:** The Culture of Sexual Assault among College Students
    General Purpose:
    Specific Purpose:

    Central Idea:

[2] **Topic:** Airport Security
    General Purpose:
    Specific Purpose:

    Central Idea:

[3] **Topic:** Distracted Driving
    General Purpose:
    Specific Purpose:

    Central Idea:

[4] **Topic:** (Your choice)
    General Purpose:
    Specific Purpose:

    Central Idea:

Developing Main Points

Objective

To practice developing main points for informative and persuasive speeches.

Instructions

Create appropriate/possible **main points** for the following hypothetical classroom speeches. For the purposes of this assignment, your responses will be based on your general knowledge.

[1] Provide **main points** for each of these speech topics: (Your general purpose can be to inform or to persuade).

    A. Learning Disabilities

    B. Hurricane Preparedness

    C. Pain Management Techniques

    D. Body Piercing

    E. Savings Accounts

[2] Provide **main points** for each of these central ideas:

    A. When considering home ownership, you need to follow three important steps.

    B. To be successful in job interviews, prior preparation is necessary.

    C. Avoid excessive sodium in your diet because it adversely impacts your health.

    D. Competitive running has both physical and social benefits.

    E. You should buy a policy to insure your belongings whether you live in a house or an apartment.

[3]   Provide **main points** for each of these specific purpose statements:

   A.   At the end of my speech, the audience will be convinced that elective cosmetic surgery can be harmful.

   B.   At the end of my speech, the audience will agree that there are advantages in attending a community college.

   C.   At the end of my speech, the audience will be able to explain the appeal and popularity of martial arts.

   D.   At the end of my speech, the audience will be persuaded that children should be home schooled.

   E.   At the end of my speech, the audience will be able to list four techniques that can help control test anxiety.

Strategic Proofs and Language in "I Have a Dream"

Background Information

Martin Luther King, Jr.'s stirring address to civil rights marchers in Washington, DC on August 28, 1963, was named the top American political speech of the twentieth century. The Mall, where the speech was delivered, is in the heart of the nation's capital. It is 2 ¼ miles of green grass and stretches from the Capitol Building to the Lincoln Memorial. Dr. King stood on the steps of the Lincoln Memorial and delivered his speech to over 200,000 marchers standing in the Mall and to millions of viewers watching on television.

Instructions

Watch the recording of Martin Luther King, Jr.'s "I Have a Dream" speech in the SCC or online. Using a manuscript of the speech (provided by your instructor), answer the following questions.

- **Identify one example of each of Aristotle's strategic proofs:**

Logos (logic) — _____

_____

Pathos (emotion) — _____

_____

Ethos (ethics) — _____

_____

Mythos (tradition) — _____

_____

- **Identify one example of each of the following:**

1. metaphor: _____

2. simile: _____

3. alliteration: _____

4. antithesis: _____

5. parallelism: _____

- **Finish the following repetitive statements in the speech:**

1. One_____ _____ later . . .

2. We can _____ _____ _____ *(but)*

3. I have _____ _____ . . . *(that)*

4. With this _____ . . . (together) . . . *(we can)*

5. Let _____ _____ . . . *(and be)*

6. _____ at last!

Identifying Organizational Patterns

Objective

To identify the most appropriate organizational patterns for informative speeches.

Instructions

Next to the specific purpose statement, put the letter(s) of the organizational pattern which would best fit the speech.

"C"	Chronological	"P-S"	Problem-solution
"T"	Topical	"C-E"	Cause and effect
"S"	Spatial		

____ [1] At the end of my speech, the audience will be able to describe the design of an ancient Egyptian pyramid.

____ [2] At the end of my speech, the audience will be able to explain how to buy a good used car.

____ [3] At the end of my speech, the audience will be able to dance the steps of a simple Irish folk dance.

____ [4] At the end of my speech, the audience will be able to list the dangers of adopting wild animals.

____ [5] At the end of my speech, the audience will be able to explain the history of comic books.

____ [6] At the end of my speech, the audience will be able to describe the steps to make the Hawaiian food, poi.

____ [7] At the end of my speech, my audience will be able to explain how safe driving is impacted by distracted driving.

____ [8] At the end of my speech, the audience will be able to explain ways to find cheaper airline tickets to combat rising flight prices.

____ [9] At the end of my speech, the audience will be able to define the ways a person can reduce stress through meditation.

____ [10] At the end of my speech, the audience will be able to list the advantages of driving an electric car to eliminate dependency on fossil fuels.

____ [11] At the end of my speech, the audience will be able to explain how to survive if stranded in the wilderness.

____ [12] At the end of my speech, the audience will be able to explain how fraudulent accident reports affect their insurance rates.

Fallacies in Reasoning

Objective

To identify common fallacies in reasoning.

Instructions

Refer to the following list of fallacies in reasoning (each defined in your public speaking text or by your instructor) and identify them in the statements below. It is possible that a statement might accurately reflect more than one fallacy. Remember that you will be a more effective and ethical persuasive speaker and listener if you *avoid* these common fallacies.

a. **Causal Fallacy (False Cause)**
b. **Bandwagon Fallacy**
c. **Either/Or Fallacy**
d. **Hasty Generalization**
e. **Slippery Slope**

f. **Ad Hominem**
g. **Red Herring**
h. **Appeal to Misplaced Authority**
i. **Non Sequitur**
j. **Sweeping Generalization**

_____ [1] In all schools across the nation, violence is on the increase.

_____ [2] If we let our middle school daughters wear make-up, the next thing you know they will want to stay out all night.

_____ [3] The quality of education in our public schools has been declining for years. Clearly, our teachers just are not doing as good of a job as teachers in the past.

_____ [4] Everybody talks about handgun accidents, but think how many people are killed each year in auto accidents. Why don't we ban automobiles?

_____ [5] Every time I wash my car, it rains.

_____ [6] The fortune in my fortune cookie said "You will travel over a great sea," so I am convinced that I'll win the online travel contest I entered for a free trip to Paris.

_____ [7] Fifty percent of Del Mar College students signed a petition in favor of offering free child care for students who have young children, so you ought to sign the petition too.

_____ [8] When guns are outlawed, only outlaws will have guns.

_____ [9] British movies are really dull. I saw two different British movies in a film class, and I nearly fell asleep during both of them.

_____ [10] Giving up our nuclear arsenal in the 1980's weakened the United States military. Giving up nuclear weapons also weakened China in the 1990's. For this reason, it is wrong to try to outlaw pistols and rifles in the United States today.

_____ [11] The witness claims that Mr. Bradley was with her that night, but she cannot be trusted because she is a friend of Mr. Bradley's.

_____ [12] If abortion were legalized, babies would be killed left and right, hundreds more people would contract STDs, and the cost of medical benefits would rise for all of us.

_____ [13] How can the deforestation of large areas of the rain forest be so bad when there are so many uses for the wood?

_____ [14] Either you go away from home to attend college, or you'll never learn to be independent.

Visual Aids

Tips for Using Visual Aids

- Choose visuals that relate directly to your speech.
- Any visual must elaborate or clarify speech content. Avoid visual aids that do not elaborate or clarify. (A can of chewing tobacco, for instance, does not make clearer for the audience the dangers of tobacco use. All audience members have seen a can of chewing tobacco.)
- Do not bring visual aids that violate college policy (no weapons, wild animals, alcohol, drug paraphernalia).
- Avoid large or cumbersome visuals. (We once had a student who brought her microwave oven. Another tried to bring his motorcycle into the classroom!)
- Display your visual aids at the proper time. If possible, keep them covered or concealed until you need them. Otherwise, they may prove distracting to your audience.
- Keep your visual aid visible. Don't stand in front of it when you are referring to it. When displaying a small visual, be sure you hold it so all can see.
- Use your visual, then put it aside. Don't fidget with your aid.
- Before deciding to use your visual aid, ask yourself this question: "Would I feel comfortable using this aid in front of a group of professionals?" If your answer is, "NO," upgrade the visual.
- The strength of a visual aid lies in the context in which it is used. No matter how powerful a photograph, chart, or movie clip may be, the audience will be less interested in merely gazing at it than discovering how you will relate it to a specific point. Even if visual aids are superior in quality, if they are poorly related to the speech, listeners will be turned off.
- Visual aids should be used to supplement rather than to serve as the main source of your speech ideas.

Why Should You Use Visual Aids?

Speaker Benefits

- You appear more professional.
- Your presentation is more dynamic.
- You are perceived as a more credible speaker.
- You are more persuasive (43 percent more likely to have your goals accepted).

Audience Benefits

- Your presentation is likely to be organized, and therefore easier for the audience to understand.
- Since visual aids take less time than verbal explanations to clarify some concepts, more information can be received and understood by the audience in the same time period.
- Research supports that the use of visual aids increases audience members' retention (ability to remember material).

Tips for Making Visual Aids

Posters and Computer Graphics

- Limit ideas to one thought per line.
- Use no more than 6 to 7 words per line
- Use no more than 6 to 7 lines per poster/screen.
- Use parallel construction to list main points and subpoints.
- Avoid large blank spaces.
- Leave a consistent margin around the perimeter of the visual.

Art

- Use art to add humor and interest.
- Relate art to content. Avoid clip art, pictures, and designs if they aren't topic specific.
- Exercise restraint. Too much art can distract from the message.
- Images should be large enough to be clearly seen from the back of the room.

Color

- Use light text on a dark background; dark text on a light background.
- Use a limited number of colors.
- Use colors that don't "fight" against each other.
- Use color to highlight, not to confuse.
- Use one color for titles and another color for text.
- Use colors consistently.

Fonts and Lettering

- Use lettering or font size consistently for titles, subtitles, and text.
- Use lettering or fonts that are large enough to be easily read by audience members in the back of the room.
- Use fonts that are easy to read.
- Avoid fancy, decorative fonts.
- Make title fonts larger than text fonts.
- Use spell check to avoid misspelled words.

Graphs and Charts

- Choose the appropriate type of graph or chart.
- Round off long numbers.
- Design any wording so audience members' eyes read left to right.
- Write all words horizontally.
- Keep your graph clear and easy to understand. If it takes longer than thirty seconds for someone to look at and understand your graph, you have made the graph too complex.

Basic PowerPoint Requirements

All students need to follow these guidelines when creating their slideshows:

Number of Slides

- Don't use your PowerPoint as your speech note cards.
- For a five to seven minute speech you should avoid an excessive amount of slides (i.e., 10+). Hit key points.

Blank/Title Slides

- Use a blank slide or a title slide at the beginning of your slideshow.
- If you use a title slide, it can have the title of your presentation on it but usually does not include your name, the date, and your class time.
- Insert a blank slide at the end of your slideshow. It should be the same background color that you have used throughout the slideshow.
- Utilize a blank screen whenever there is a time lapse between the information to be presented from one slide to the next.

Color

- Don't overuse. Be consistent with the same background color for each screen.
- When using a template (wallpaper background), make sure it is appropriate for the speech topic.
- Choose one color for titles and a separate color for text (unless instructed otherwise by your instructor).
- Maintain consistency in color of fonts.
- Choose a color for letters that contrasts with the slide's background (dark-colored letters on pale/light backgrounds and light-colored letters on dark backgrounds).

Fonts and Spacing

- Maintain consistency in choice of font (make sure it is not a font that is difficult to read/see).
- Size of font needs to be large enough for entire audience in the back of the room to see (minimum of 44–point for titles and 32–point for text).
- Boldface fonts if they are not already bold.
- Follow the "6–7 words/6–7 lines" rule to avoid a screen that is too busy or crowded.
- Maintain consistency in capitalization for titles and text.
- Use upper and lower case lettering (not all caps) for all titles and text.
- Maintain consistency in spacing.
- Frame/border your pictures/art when appropriate.
- Avoid too much blank space on slides.
- Align bullet points. Do not center them.
- Maintain even margins.
- Do not overlap letters and pictures. Words become difficult to read.

Wording

- Use phrases (not full sentences) for your text.
- Use parallel structure.
- Use correct grammar and spelling. Utilize the grammar and spelling checker.

Visual Images

- Use images related/appropriate to speech content.
- Use clip art, pictures, charts, etc. that are clear (not fuzzy) and large enough to be seen in the back of the classroom.
- Don't overuse visual images; avoid too many images on one slide. One good picture or drawing is usually sufficient. Two images/pictures are the limit on a single slide.
- Leave a margin around the edge of slides.
- Do not put text too close to pictures/images.
- Do not use cartoons or images that have a watermark stamp on them.
- Crop copyright information from pictures and images.

Animation and Sound

- Avoid distracting animation.
- Do not use sound unless you have incorporated streaming video.
- Adjust volume for streaming video so it is loud and clear.

Transitions and Custom Animation

- Use appropriate/non-distracting transitions and maintain consistency between every slide.
- Use "custom animation" when appropriate and be consistent in the form chosen (bring in one piece of bulleted information/full phrase at a time).

Researching

Tips for Online Researching

Purpose

To teach students 1. the value of logical operators and 2. to be more critical consumers of the Internet.

Background information:

An area of importance to Web users interested in conducting more effective and efficient searches is the utilization of **logical operators**, which are key words and quotation marks.

Keywords

Most people conduct searches use only a few key words in their searches—rather than multiple key words.

It is better to use more key words than fewer when searching online. Some computer experts suggest that it may be necessary to use as many as a dozen key words to effectively limit a search to a manageable amount of information. Each keyword cuts down the number of erroneous matches, and if you use enough, you can cut out almost all of the irrelevant "stuff."

Example:

You are interested in discovering if and how racial profiling affects Hispanics in Texas.

Keywords:

Too broad:	Racial profiling
Better:	Racial profiling Texas
Best:	Racial profiling Texas Hispanics

(Several reliable articles come to the top of the search list with these four key words.)

Example:

You would like to know more about a famous Bavarian castle. You know it was built by King Ludwig.

Keywords:

Too broad: Bavaria
Better: Bavaria castle
Best: Bavaria castle King Ludwig

(The first entry on the search list takes you to Neuschwanstein Castle, Ludwig's most famous, but other entries discuss his two other castles.)

Example:

You are researching a speech about breast cancer in men, and you want to know the symptoms.

Keywords:

Too broad: breast cancer
Better: breast cancer in men
Best: symptoms breast cancer in men

Quotation marks

By putting words into "quotation marks," users are telling their search engines to look for the exact phrase entered. The only articles that will come up will have the words in the exact order in which you typed them.

Oral Citations

When you give a speech, whether in class or to the community, you will be expected to cite your sources of information. You are familiar with this practice when you write a research paper and include a "works cited" page. In public speaking, you orally cite the sources from which you gathered the information for your speech. Audiences will base your credibility as a speaker partly upon the credibility and the recency of the sources you cite. Here are some examples to look over as you plan your speech:

Direct Quotation

I had an interview on April 14 with Paula Medina, a real estate agent for the past ten years with Keller-Williams in Corpus Christi. Ms. Medina said, "There are presently 2,710 properties in foreclosure in our city. Many of these were owned by persons who had unsuccessfully tried to sell their homes before the homes went into foreclosure."

The world's only known pirate shipwreck is the *Whydah* which sank off the coast of New England in April, 1717. On the website of *National Geographic* which I accessed on August 12, 2015, I discovered that historians have learned a great deal from this shipwreck. For instance, "the abundance of metal buttons, cuff links, collar stays, rings, neck chains, and square belt buckles scattered on the seafloor shows that the pirates were far more sophisticated—even dandyish—in their dress than was previously thought. This was an act of defiance—similar in spirit, perhaps, to today's rock stars."

Indirect (Paraphrased) Quotation

Should community colleges come without a tuition bill? The editors of the magazine *Scientific American* think so. Their August 14, 2014, article, "Why Community Colleges Should Be Free," which I accessed at the magazine's website on September 12, 2015, states that community colleges are pillars of STEM (science, technology, engineering and mathematics) education. They train technicians for jobs in leading-edge industries. In addition, community colleges serve as gateways for the underrepresented and the working class.

In his 2012 book, *The Power of Habit,* award-winning business reporter, Charles Duhigg, writes that most of the choices we make may feel like decision-making, but they're not. They're habits. Meals we order, what we say to our kids when we put them to bed each night, whether or not we spend or save, how often we exercise, how often we have a beer. At one point they were conscious decisions, but then the behavior became automatic. Duhigg believes that when we understand how and why that happens, we can rebuild those patterns in whichever way we choose.

Guidelines for Using Oral Citations

[1] Oral citations should be used to document information in your speech that you are using from books, magazines, newspapers, the Internet, interviews, TV shows, online databases, etc. Make the documentation specific by using exact names, dates, and publications.

[2] If the source is unfamiliar to your audience, establish his/her/its credibility for your audience.

[3] When quoting or paraphrasing information from a book, tell your audience the title, author, and year of publication.

[4] When quoting or paraphrasing information from a magazine, journal, or newspaper, tell your audience the name of the publication, date published, article title, and author.

[5] When using information from an interview, tell your audience the name of the person interviewed, the date of the interview, and the credentials of the interviewee to establish his/her credibility on the topic.

[6] When using information from an Internet source, tell your audience the name of the web site (the sponsoring organization), the date you accessed the site. Give other information like article title, author, etc., if available. *Do not* include an Internet address or URL.

[7] Don't make your oral citations too wordy. Avoid such things as cities where books are published, pages you read in a periodical, edition and volume numbers, etc.

[8] If you are quoting a person but have taken the quotation from a print or Internet source, give your audience the print or Internet source also. If you neglect to do so, it sounds to your audience like you have personally interviewed the person.

[9] If you are repeating a source that you have previously cited in your speech, you do not need to repeat the whole oral citation. In this circumstance, you can make a brief reference back to the source. Example: In the *New York Times* article I previously cited, the President was quoted as saying, "… ."

Oral Citation Exercise

Identify the mistakes in the following examples. If there is no error, write "no mistake."

[1] I saw some guy on TV last week who said that strawberries grow better in South Texas in the late summer than in the spring.

_____

[2] The Houston Texans are the second franchise to have emerged from Houston. The Texans formed in 2002 after the Houston Oilers moved to Nashville, Tennessee. The Houston Texans began play on September 8, 2002 against the Dallas Cowboys. They stunned the Cowboys 19-10, and became only the second NFL expansion in history to win their first game. They lost the next five games.

_____

[3] When I spoke to Gary Schmelling, he told me that the motto of Hyatt Resorts is "The difference between a mere place to relax and a magnificent experience."

_____

[4] In an article titled, "The Personality Profile of a Serial Killer" by Julietta Leung, I discovered that approximately 90% of known serial killers are Caucasian males between the ages of 25 to 35.

_____

[5] In 1884, a bill passed Congress granting land to the Paiute Indians, but it was never implemented.

_____

[6] The average age of the gamer is rapidly approaching 30. As people in their 30s and 40s continue to play video games into their senior years, the genres of games will expand to accommodate those audiences and embrace their higher incomes. I found this information on May 4, 2015, on the PBS website in an article titled *The Future of Video Gaming*, by Michael Dolan. Dolan also writes that there may even be a game series that allows participants to see what it's like to perform in a real-life emergency room.

_____

[7] I remember reading that one of the reasons NBA player LeBron James left Miami and returned to the Cleveland Cavaliers in 2014 is because he and his wife are from northeastern Ohio, and they wanted to live nearer to family and friends.

_____

[8] On the website of the *Corpus Christi Caller/Times,* I read that the Texas State Aquarium has a large economic impact on our area. A recent report found the aquarium provided more than $441 million to the local economy during the past 10 years. About $48.5 million was contributed just last year.

_____

[9] According to the Internet, poet Robert Frost was the first poet in the 20th century to read a poem at a Presidential inauguration. John F. Kennedy asked Frost to be present and read his works at Kennedy's 1961 inauguration. The practice of a poetry reading continued until 2001 when George W. Bush did not have a poet at his inauguration. Barack Obama revived the tradition at his inaugural in 2009.

_____

[10] On April 11, 2015, I accessed http://time.com/3818487/malala-yousafzai-asteroid/ and read an article titled *Teen Activist Malala Yousafzai Gets Her Own Asteroid.* Amy Mainzer, the NASA astronomer who discovered the rock, was the one who named it after Yousafzai. Mainzer said that it was brought to her attention that although many asteroids have been named, very few have been named to honor the contributions of women (and particularly women of color). In October 2012, after Yousafzai (then 14) blogged about her determination to become a doctor, a Taliban gunman shot her as she boarded a school bus in Pakistan's Swat Valley. Yousafzai now works with her foundation to empower girls through education and is the recipient of the Nobel Peace Prize.

_____

[11] *Night,* a novel of living through the Holocaust, was written by Elie Wiesel in 1972. In 2006, Wiesel's wife, Marion, translated a new version in which Elie wrote a new forward for the novel. In it, he states that he wrote the book because "… convinced that this period in history would be judged one day, I knew that I must bear witness."

_____

[12] I recently read online some very important words from Eleanor Roosevelt. The former First Lady said about international conflict, "I cannot believe that war is the best solution. No one won the last war, and no one will win the next war."

_____

Name _____

Class Time _____

Oral Citation Practice

Oral citations are used to document information that comes from a source other than yourself. In other words, you need to document every "borrowed" word. Some examples of these sources are books, magazines/journals, newspapers, the Internet, interviews, and TV shows. Your audience will base your credibility as a speaker partly upon the credibility and the recency of the sources you cite.

Some of the most common pieces of information:

- Source (magazine/journal, book, newspaper, website, person, etc.)
- Author
- Date it was published/date of personal interview (if website, date accessed/date last updated)
- Title of article/book/web document or credentials of person interviewed
- Name of website and website sponsor (if applicable)

Instructions

Use the following suggested formats to create your oral citations.

Book:

According to the _____ book, _____
                    (copyright date)   *(book title)*

written by _____, I discovered that
                              (author/s)

_____

_____

Newspaper:

In the _____ _____
              (publishing date)   *(newspaper)*

article _____, author, _____
                (article title)   *(author/s if provided)*

stated that _____

_____

Journal, Magazine, Periodical:

In the _____ article _____
         (date published)   *(article title)*

found in (the)_____, author/s _____
               (journal/magazine title)   *(author/s)*

write that _____

_____

Website:

On the website _____, I found a document
                                  (title of website)

titled _____ . This website was
                              (document title)

last updated on _____ **(or)** was accessed on _____ . (Provide one.)
               (date)   *(date you accessed information)*

(If applicable) This article/document was written by _____
                                           (author/s—if provided)

on _____ . The information I discovered is that _____
    (date)

_____

Interview:

*This group activity doesn't include an interview; this is the format to use for information you gain from an interview.

On _____ I interviewed _____
            (date)   *(individual's name)*

He/she is _____
                           (credentials—position, experience, etc.)

From him/her I learned that _____

_____

Important Researching Rules for Informative and Persuasive Speeches

[1] When researching for your INFORMATIVE and PERSUASIVE SPEECHES, start your search for information with online library databases. They are going to have the most credible sources.

[2] To access the library databases on computers when you are off campus, go to the Del Mar website and find the library or go directly to the library website (library.delmar.edu). Use the following user name and password: User name: delmar; Password: _____ (changes every semester—ask your instructor or library staff).

[3] If you use information for your speech from the Internet, you will need to make sure that you assess the credibility of those sources. Look first at the domain (the last three letters of the URL). Then look for the author of the site or the author of the specific article/document on the site that you intend to use. You may need to research the author to discover what makes him/her credible on the topic. You should also look to see if the website has a sponsoring organization that can give the source credibility. Lastly, make sure that all the research sources you use for your speech are not biased and are current.

[4] Don't use encyclopedias or Wikipedia as research sources. Encyclopedia entries are general and relatively brief. Wikipedia can be altered by anyone and is not considered a credible source.

[5] Don't use abstracts of periodical articles. Abstracts are short summaries of an article. Use only full text articles as a source.

[6] Remember that you are required to have a minimum of three DIFFERENT sources for your INFORMATIVE and PERSUASIVE SPEECHES. THIS DOES NOT MEAN CITE ONE SOURCE THREE TIMES. Each source used in your speech needs to be cited aloud. These oral citations should follow the guidelines in this activity book. You can also use the fill-in-the-blank format in this book. Your oral citations are a part of your speech grade. (See the grade/speech critique form that your instructor will use to evaluate your speech.)

[7] List all of the research sources you use for the content of your speech in your bibliography/works cited sheet. Attach the sheet to your speech outline. List the sources using the MLA (Modern Language Association) or APA (American Language Association) format. Check with your instructor for the format he/she requires. You can go to several online sites to help you write your source information in the correct format (i.e., citationmachine.net or easybib.com). On the site, you will be asked to identify the type of source you are using (book, periodical, website, etc.). Indicate either MLA or APA format. You will be presented with specific questions. After you enter the answers, the website will put the source into the correct format. Cut and paste those three sources into your bibliography/works cited, and list them alphabetically.

Informative
Speaking

Key Concepts of Informative Speaking

Objectives

- To create a desire for information by arousing the audience's interest in the information
- To present information so that it will be clearly understood
- To help the audience retain or remember the information presented
- To open new doors on how the presented information can be utilized

Types of Informative Speeches

- Speeches about objects
- Speeches about procedures
- Speeches about people
- Speeches about ideas
- Speeches about events

Informative Organizational Patterns/Formats

[1] **CHRONOLOGICAL** format explains steps in a process or in ordering ideas in a specific time sequence. (Example: speech explaining steps in starting a small business.)

[2] **SPATIAL** format arranges main points according to their relationship in space. (Example: speech describing the possible locations for a high-rise parking garage on campus might move from the north side of the campus to the middle and then to the south.)

[3] **TOPICAL** format identifies main points or key components which elaborate on the central idea and divide into natural divisions. (Example: speech about Attention Deficit Disorder could be organized into various forms of treatment such as medication, psychological counseling, and educational interventions.)

[4] **CAUSE/EFFECT** format arranges speech information tracing a condition or action from its courses to its effects or from effects back to causes. (Example: speech about Alzheimer's Disease could be divided by first dealing with the causes of the condition and then addressing symptoms/effects.)

[5] **PROBLEM-SOLUTION** format educates the audience about a specific problem and then informs the audience about actual or possible solutions. (Example: speech on beach trash could elaborate on the problem and then explain how the problem is currently being addressed.)

The Informative Speech

Your goal for this speech is to give new information to your listeners and help them understand and remember it. The major questions your audience should be able to answer are: Did we learn something new? Do we understand something new or did we learn something in a different manner? The topic for this speech may be selected from any area of your knowledge or experience. It can be a topic you already know quite a bit about and that you can make interesting to your classmates. *You must supplement your knowledge with extensive information derived from research.* Your topic should cover only one major idea that can be thoroughly covered in the time allotted. However, the key to a successful speech is to carefully choose your topic so that it is narrow enough to cover adequately with the necessary details. Your audience should also know why you think it is worth their time to listen to your presentation. Prepare your audience to learn something new with a well-planned introduction. In the conclusion, use tools that help to reinforce the information. Deliver your speech in an easy to understand, organized manner, and then wrap up the presentation so that it will be remembered.

Specific Speech Requirements

- Must meet time requirements set by your instructor.
- Extemporaneous delivery
- Notecards required for delivery (using key words and phrases)
- Typed outline (meeting your instructor's specifications)
- Minimum of three current, credible sources cited within your speech (following guidelines for oral citations)
- Visual aid may be required (following the guidelines in your text and this activity book)
- Practice, practice, practice

When preparing and practicing your presentation, ask yourself the following questions:

- Did I spend adequate time researching? Last minute preparation is usually not successful.
- Did I practice my completed speech with my visual aid, timing myself so that I can feel assured that my speech length is between five to seven minutes?
- Did I read "Criteria for Grading Speeches" in this activity manual on pages 9–10, becoming completely familiar with how my presentation will be evaluated?

Topics for Informative Speeches

The following are general topics used by former Del Mar students in public speaking classes. Use this list as a "jumpstart" to come up with a topic idea for your informative speech.

- Medical treatments for lung cancer
- Hot checks—what happens when you have insufficient funds
- Ways to prevent back injuries
- Programs offered by Metro Ministries
- The advantages of being bilingual
- Three things you should know about fishing for redfish
- The difference between right and left brain orientation
- When your child has sickle-cell anemia
- Tips on selecting a day care center
- Selecting athletic footwear to suit your sport
- Bound for Broadway—what to do to get there
- The signs and symptoms of child abuse
- The stages of grief
- Planting and caring for an herb garden
- Special issues for single dads
- Reactive Attachment Disorder: What happens when a child never learns to bond
- How police and courts handle juvenile offenders
- What it takes to become an Eagle Scout
- Scoliosis: A hidden disability
- Jalisco Dancing
- Spinal Cord Injury
- Native American traditions in the Cherokee Nation
- Haunted locations in Corpus Christi
- Signs and symptoms of domestic abuse
- Warning signs of suicide
- Organic pest control: an alternative to pesticides

- A history of martial arts films
- The incredible intelligence of bees
- Date rape—It could happen to you
- Cochlear implants for the deaf
- The search for Atlantis
- The traditions of the Chinese New Year
- The history of Del Mar College
- Migraine headaches
- The evolution of whales
- Japanese fighting dogs: the Yokozuna Tosa
- The history of the game of pool
- The body and mind benefits of yoga
- Treatments for back pain
- Why families go abroad to adopt
- Read your palm and learn your future
- What to consider before having plastic surgery
- Gum disease prevention
- Ways to safeguard your identity on the Internet
- Causes of kleptomania
- Your dreams and what they mean
- Techniques to improve your memory
- Effective uses of hypnotism
- Sam Houston
- Principles of Wicca
- Mahatma Gandhi and Civil Disobedience
- Microbiotic Diet
- Obsessive Compulsive Disorder
- Broken Heart Syndrome
- Safeguards for Internet Dating

Speech 1315

INFORMATIVE SPEAKING

Name _____

Class Time _____

Informative Speech Topic Declaration

TOPIC: _____

GENERAL PURPOSE: _____

SPECIFIC PURPOSE: _____

_____

_____

_____

_____

MAIN POINTS: I. _____

          II. _____

          III. _____

CENTRAL IDEA/THESIS STATEMENT: _____

_____

_____

_____

CIRCLE THE ORGANIZATIONAL PATTERN/FORMAT YOU PLAN ON USING:

topical   chronological   cause/effect   problem-solution   spatial

Unless notified by your instructor that your topic is inappropriate or ineffective, this sheet COMMITS you to this declared topic. You cannot change your topic without approval from your instructor.

Name _Example_

Class Time _____

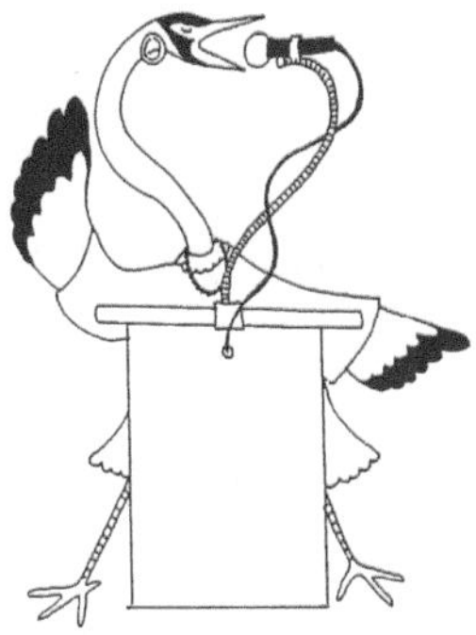

Informative Speech Topic Declaration

TOPIC: _Medical Uses for Botox_

GENERAL PURPOSE: _To inform_

SPECIFIC PURPOSE: _At the end of my speech, the audience will be able to list the medical uses for botox._

MAIN POINTS: I. _Reduce severe headaches_

            II. _Reduce symptoms of excessive sweating_

            III. _Treat incontinence_

CENTRAL IDEA/THESIS STATEMENT: _Botox is used to reduce severe headaches, reduce symptoms of excessive sweating, and treat incontinence._

CIRCLE THE ORGANIZATIONAL PATTERN/FORMAT YOU PLAN ON USING:

(topical)   chronological   cause/effect   problem-solution   spatial

Unless notified by your instructor that your topic is inappropriate or ineffective, this sheet COMMITS you to this declared topic. You cannot change your topic without approval from your instructor.

Speech 1315 Name Example

INFORMATIVE SPEAKING Class Time

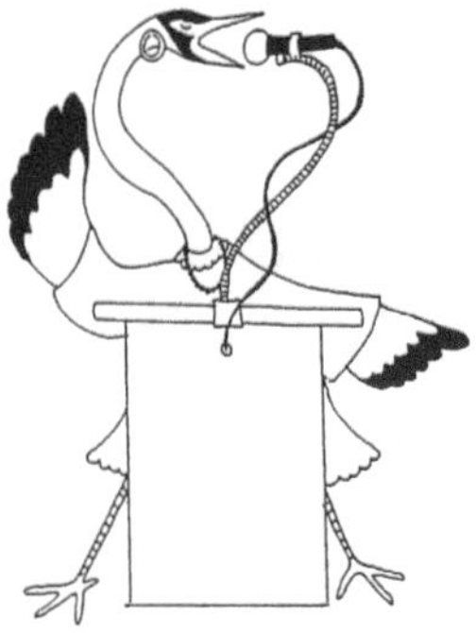

Informative Speech Topic Declaration

TOPIC: Martin Luther King, Jr. and the Montgomery Bus Boycott

GENERAL PURPOSE: To inform

SPECIFIC PURPOSE: At the end of my speech, the audience will be able to explain the involvement of Dr. Martin Luther King, Jr. in the Montgomery bus boycott.

MAIN POINTS:

I. Background of the bus boycott

II. Events of the bus boycott

III. Long-term results of the bus boycott

CENTRAL IDEA/THESIS STATEMENT: Martin Luther King, Jr. was vital to the planning, the execution, and the long-term results of the Montgomery bus boycott.

CIRCLE THE ORGANIZATIONAL PATTERN/FORMAT YOU PLAN ON USING:

topical (chronological) cause/effect problem-solution spatial

Unless notified by your instructor that your topic is inappropriate or ineffective, this sheet COMMITS you to this declared topic. You cannot change your topic without approval from your instructor.

Topics for "How To" Speeches

Demonstration and Process

Demonstration Topics

- How to saddle a horse
- How to make hemp jewelry
- How to prepare a sushi roll
- How to make a scrapbook page
- How to set a table for formal dining
- How to clean crabs for cooking
- How to wrap a gift
- How to pack a suitcase
- How to make frittata
- How to make gift baskets
- How to apply stage makeup
- How to play simple guitar chords
- How to write a Haiku poem
- How to decorate a cake
- How to properly lift weights
- How to perform the Heimlich Maneuver
- How to ring bells in a hand bell choir
- How to tile

Process Topics

- How to make a quilt
- How to write a resume
- How to prepare for an interview
- How mammals are trained to do tricks at Sea World
- How to find an apartment
- How to change the oil in your car
- How to apply for financial aid
- How to plan for a camping trip
- How to plan a wedding
- How to barbeque steaks
- How to write a song
- How to set up a web page
- How to design an exercise plan
- How to stain wood
- How to wash and wax your car
- How to buy a used car
- How to make an oriental rug
- How to trim a tree

Name _____

Class Time _____

Process/Demonstration Speech Topic Declaration

TOPIC: _____

GENERAL PURPOSE: _____

SPECIFIC PURPOSE: _____

_____

MAIN POINTS: 1. _____

2. _____

3. _____

CENTRAL IDEA/THESIS STATEMENT: (Introduce the topic and the overall focus of your message. What is your topic, its focus, and why is it important for your audience? Write this statement as you will actually say it in the speech.)

_____

_____

_____

PREVIEW STATEMENT: (Combine the topic and the titles of the three main points into one concise sentence that will establish the message sequence for your audience. Write this statement as you will actually say it in the speech.)

_____

_____

_____

DESCRIPTION OF VISUAL AIDS TO BE USED:

_____

ANTICIPATED OUTCOME OF YOUR MESSAGE:

_____

_____

_____

Unless notified by your instructor that your topic is inappropriate or ineffective, this sheet COMMITS you to this declared topic. You cannot change your topic without approval from your instructor.

Name *Example*

Class Time _____

Demonstration Speech Topic Declaration

TOPIC: *How to Putt a Golf Ball*

GENERAL PURPOSE: *To inform*

SPECIFIC PURPOSE: *At the end of my speech, the audience will be able to putt a golf ball.*

MAIN POINTS: 1. *Aim straight at the hole*

2. *Visualize the path the ball will take into the hole*

3. *Hold your breath and don't move while taking your shot*

CENTRAL IDEA/THESIS STATEMENT: (Introduce the topic and the overall focus of your message. What is your topic, its focus, and why is it important for your audience? Write this statement as you will actually say it in the speech.)

There are three main steps to follow when putting a golf ball.

PREVIEW STATEMENT: (Combine the topic and the titles of the three main points into one concise sentence that will establish the message sequence for your audience. Write this statement as you will actually say it in the speech.)

Today I will demonstrate the three most important steps to take when putting a golf ball—aim, visualize, and keep your body still.

DESCRIPTION OF VISUAL AIDS TO BE USED:

Golf clubs, golf ball, portable putting green

ANTICIPATED OUTCOME OF YOUR MESSAGE:

My audience will be able to putt a golf ball.

Unless notified by your instructor that your topic is inappropriate or ineffective, this sheet COMMITS you to this declared topic. You cannot change your topic without approval from your instructor.

Name *Example*

Class Time _____

Process Speech Topic Declaration

TOPIC: *Fire! How to Save Your Life*

GENERAL PURPOSE: *To inform*

SPECIFIC PURPOSE: *At the end of my speech, the audience will be able list the steps in planning an escape from their living quarters in case of a fire.*

MAIN POINTS:

1. *Draw the floor plan of your home or apartment*

2. *Identify two exists for each room*

3. *Decide on a waiting place where everyone will meet*

4. *Practice your exit plan until it becomes automatic*

CENTRAL IDEA/THESIS STATEMENT: (Introduce the topic and the overall focus of your message. What is your topic, its focus, and why is it important for your audience? Write this statement as you will actually say it in the speech.)

There are four steps to follow when planning a fire escape for your home or apartment.

PREVIEW STATEMENT: (Combine the topic and the titles of the three main points into one concise sentence that will establish the message sequence for your audience. Write this statement as you will actually say it in the speech.)

To exit safely from your home or apartment in case of a fire, you need to draw the floor plan, know two ways out of every room, decide on a waiting place to meet after exiting, and practice your escape plan.

DESCRIPTION OF VISUAL AIDS TO BE USED:

Power Point slide show displaying a sample floor plan of a home or apartment, identifying two possible exits for each room

ANTICIPATED OUTCOME OF YOUR MESSAGE:

My audience will be able to plan escape routes if a fire ever occurs in their home or apartment.

Unless notified by your instructor that your topic is inappropriate or ineffective, this sheet COMMITS you to this declared topic. You cannot change your topic without approval from your instructor.

Guide for Informative Preparation Outline (Format #1)

Guide for Full-Sentence Preparation Outline (Check with your instructor for the outline format he/she prefers.)

Use the following guide to develop your preparation outline for your INFORMATIVE Speech. This sample guide has three main points in the body of the speech. In your speech, the number and the organization of main points, subpoints, and sub-subpoints will vary depending on the topic and purpose of your speech. However, the elements needed in the outline—title, specific purpose statement, central idea, introduction, body, conclusion, transition statements, visual aids, and bibliography—will remain the same. **For more information check your textbook and refer to the Del Mar student's informative speech in this activity book.** Write out your introduction and conclusion in its entirety (using Roman numerals I and II to indicate attention getting material and orienting material in your introduction and Roman numeral I and II for the summary statement and the clincher technique in your conclusion). The body of your speech will then indicate main points and subpoints (utilizing Roman numerals for main points and capital letters for subpoints, etc.) with information that is formulated in one full sentence per outline symbol.

Name:_____

Date:_____

Course Time:_____

TITLE
(This should be your speech title.)

GENERAL PURPOSE: To inform

SPECIFIC PURPOSE: (Should fit the requirements for specific purpose statements—check textbook.)

CENTRAL IDEA: (Should fit the requirements for central ideas—check textbook.)

INTRODUCTION:

I. (Write out your entire speech introduction, but put all of your **"attention getting material"** under Roman Numeral I—be creative—using one or more of the following techniques: tell a hypothetical story or a personal narrative, use a quote, arouse curiosity, use an illustration or an example, present startling information, use a visual aid, or do a demonstration.)

II. (Write out the **"orienting material"** portion of your introduction … and put it all under Roman Numeral II. This portion should include: **your link and/or credibility** toward your speech subject (unless you have used a narrative in your attention getter and then this function may have been already satisfied), **the common ground you have with your audience** (the audience's link to the speech subject—what's in it for them), **background information** (if necessary … defining terms etc.), and the **central idea statement** (this should clearly preview main points of your speech).

BODY:

I. Use a single complete sentence to express the main point of this section of the speech.

    A. Subpoint (As with main points, all subpoints should be written in full sentences.)

        1. Sub-sub-point (This should also be one complete sentence.)

        2. Sub-sub-point (This should also be one complete sentence.)

    B. Subpoint

Transition statement: (One full sentence helps the audience move from one point of your speech to the next. Use transitions, signposts, internal reviews/previews, etc. Check textbook for examples.)

II. Use a single complete sentence to express the main point of this section of the speech.

    A. Subpoint

    B. Subpoint

        1. Sub-sub-point

            a. Sub-sub-sub-point

            b. Sub-sub-sub-point

        2. Sub-sub-point

Transition statement: (One full sentence helps the audience to move from your second main point to the third main point of your speech.)

III. Use a single complete sentence to express the main point of this section of the speech.

    A. Subpoint

        1. Sub-sub-point

        2. Sub-sub-point

    B. Subpoint

        1. Sub-sub-point

        2. Sub-sub-point

        3. Sub-sub-point

CONCLUSION:

I. (Your conclusion should be written out word for word as you intend to say it in your speech. Your **summary statement,** which is basically a re-wording of your central idea statement, should be written out under Roman Numeral I.)

II. (Your **clincher** should use one of the following strong ending techniques: (end with an appropriate quote, an example or illustration, a visual that has impact, or a reference back to something mentioned in your introduction. It should be written out under Roman Numeral II.)

VISUAL AIDS:

This should be a specific listing of your visual aid(s). For instance, don't just write "PowerPoint." Indicate what you are planning or at least thinking about including in the slide show.

BIBLIOGRAPHY:

Here is where you list complete citations for the research materials you used in preparing your speech. You are to use MLA format (Modern Language Association) or APA format (American Psychological Association). Check with your instructor on his/her requirement. Example bibliographic formats can be found on the Del Mar Library web site. Remember bibliographic entries should be listed in alphabetical order by author, and then if no author is available, by title/document. Use correct indentation and punctuation.

IMPORTANT POINTS TO REMEMBER WHEN COMPLETING YOUR OUTLINE:

[1] Material placed in a complete sentence outline should be worded so that each sentence carries the gist, or essence, of that material.

[2] At the top of the first page, write the speech title. Then follow that with the general purpose, specific purpose, and the central idea of the speech (labeling each).

[3] Divide the rest of your outline into three distinct parts, capitalizing the words: INTRODUCTION, BODY, and CONCLUSION.

[4] Use the standard outline symbols: I, II, III; A, B, C; 1, 2, 3; a, b, c; etc.

[5] Indent each symbol by placing it under the first word of the sentence it follows; never allow any sentence or part of a sentence to extend to the left hand margin as far as the symbols do.

[6] Follow each symbol with one declarative sentence, not a question.

[7] Use only two or three main points in the body of a short five to seven minute speech.

[8] Main points and sub-points should be carefully worded to conform to a consistent organizational pattern, should be of equal importance, be given equal time, and should not overlap.

Name _____

Class Time _____

Informative Preparation Outline Aid (Format #1)

This outline activity is designed to help you create a well-planned, organized informative outline. Your final preparation outline should be typed when turned in to your instructor. DO NOT TURN IN THIS FILL-IN-THE–BLANK FORM.

_____
(title of speech)

GENERAL PURPOSE: *To inform* _____

SPECIFIC PURPOSE: (same specific purpose that was on declaration after corrections were made—

BEGIN WITH): *At the end of my speech the audience will be able to explain, discuss, demonstrate,*

list, etc. _____

_____

CENTRAL IDEA: (same central idea that was on declaration after corrections were made—ONE SENTENCE that previews your main points) _____

_____

_____

INTRODUCTION

I. ATTENTION GETTING TECHNIQUE/S: (make sure to use FULL SENTENCE/S—tell a story/ hypothetical or personal narrative, question/rhetorical or overt, startling information, demonstration, use a visual)

_____

_____

_____

_____

_____

II. ORIENTING MATERIAL—includes speaker link, common ground/audience link coming from the results of your survey, background information if necessary, and central idea statement that previews the main points I, II,—USE FULL SENTENCES. *(central idea should be the same sentence as on top of outline)*

_____

_____

_____

_____

BODY: each symbol in the body of the outline-needs to be only ONE FULL SENTENCE

I. MAIN POINT: needs to be ONE FULL SENTENCE that was previewed in the central idea

_____

_____

_____

A. SUB-POINT: needs to be ONE FULL SENTENCE that clarifies or details the preceding main point

_____

_____

1. Sub-sub point: ONE SENTENCE that clarifies and/or details the preceding sub-point

_____

_____

2. Sub-sub point: ONE SENTENCE that clarifies and/or details the preceding sub-point

_____

_____

B. SUB-POINT: ONE SENTENCE clarifying or elaborating on the main point

_____

_____

1. Sub-sub point: ONE SENTENCE that details and/or clarifies the preceding sub-point

_____

_____

2. Sub-sub point; ONE SENTENCE that details and/or clarifies the preceding sub-point

_____

_____

Transition: _Now that you know_ _____

let's move on to _____

II. (MAIN POINT: should be ONE SENTENCE that has been previewed in the central idea

_____

_____

_____

    A. SUB-POINT: ONE SENTENCE that clarifies and/or details the preceding main point

_____

_____

        1. Sub-sub point: ONE SENTENCE that clarifies and/or details the preceding sub-point

_____

_____

        2. Sub-sub point: ONE SENTENCE that clarifies and/or details the preceding sub-point

_____

_____

    B. SUB-POINT: ONE SENTENCE that clarifies and/or details the preceding main point

_____

_____

1. Sub-sub point: ONE SENTENCE that clarifies and/or details the preceding sub-point

_____

_____

2. Sub-sub point: ONE SENTENCE that clarifies and/or details the preceding sub-point

_____

_____

Transition: _Now that you know_____

_let's move on to_____

III. MAIN POINT: needs to be ONE FULL SENTENCE that was previewed in the central idea

_____

_____

_____

A. SUB-POINT: needs to be ONE FULL SENTENCE that clarifies or elaborates on the preceding main point _____

_____

_____

1. Sub-sub point: ONE SENTENCE that clarifies or elaborates on the preceding sub-point

_____

_____

2. Sub-sub point: ONE SENTENCE that clarifies or elaborates on the preceding sub-point

_____

_____

B. SUB-POINT: needs to be ONE FULL SENTENCE that clarifies and/or elaborates on the preceding main point

_____

_____

1. Sub-sub point: ONE FULL SENTENCE that details the preceding sub-point

_____

_____

2. Sub-sub point: ONE FULL SENTENCE that details the preceding sub-point

_____

_____

CONCLUSION:

I. SUMMARY STATEMENT: should be a re-wording of the central idea

_____

_____

II. CLINCHER: use a specific technique: hypothetical or personal narrative, quote, demonstration, visual, connecting back to attention getter

_____

_____

_____

VISUAL AID: describe specifics of what type you are thinking of using (PowerPoint, poster, object/s, etc.) and what specifically you are planning to show.

_____

_____

WORKS CITED [listed alphabetically] (use MLA—Modern Language Association—access online to have source information formatted correctly). Check with your instructor.

Name _____

Class Time _____

Checklist for Writing an Informative Preparation Outline

(Outline—Format #1)

Check off the following items as you include them in your speech outline.

OUTLINE FORMAT

____Title written at top
____General purpose
____Specific purpose
    ____begins with "At the end of my speech …"
    ____reference to audience
    ____realistic objectives
____Central idea/thesis statement
____Consistent form used
    ____complete sentence
    ____transitions (between main points)
    ____subdivisions (minimum of two—every
        "A" needs a "B"; every "1" needs "2," etc.)

BODY

____Main points
    ____ have the appropriate number of
        main points
    ____support the specific purpose
    ____organized effectively
____Support materials
    ____uses different types of support materials
    ____contains adaquate support information

INTRODUCTION

____Attention material
    ____grabs listener's interest
____Orienting material
    ____prepares the audience for the body of
        the speech
    ____includes speaker credibility/link to topic
    ____includes audience link to topic
    ____previews the speech's main points

CONCLUSION

____"Brakelight" (signal the end)
____Summary of main points
____Avoids introducing new information
____Clincher

BIBLIOGRAPHY

____Minimum of three sources included
____Cite using proper MLA or APA form (check
    with instructor for his/her requirement)

VISUAL AID(S)

____Each listed separately (identifying content)

Example of Informative Outline (Format #1)

Alopecia

GENERAL PURPOSE: To inform

SPECIFIC PURPOSE: At the end of my speech the audience will be able to identify the different types of alopecia.

CENTRAL IDEA: Alopecia, which is an autoimmune condition, can present itself as Male Pattern Baldness, Alopecia Areata, or Alopecia Universalis.

INTRODUCTION

I.   Imagine brushing your hair and then noticing that the brush is clumped with much more hair than usual. Then a few weeks later when you shower and wash your hair, you realize how much of your hair has accumulated on the bottom drain. Before you know it, you have lost almost all of your hair in less than one year.

II. On my class survey, everyone in here said they have had a "bad hair day," but imagine what it would be like to experience "no hair days." We all know that society puts a great deal of emphasis on appearance, and in our culture much of that emphasis revolves around hair. I don't have to imagine this "no hair" scenario because at the age of six, I was diagnosed with alopecia. What I learned over the last few years is that there are different forms of this disease, with distinct characteristics. Alopecia, which is an autoimmune condition, can present itself as Adrogenetic Alopecia, Alopecia Areata, or Alopecia Universalis.

BODY

I.   Androgenetic Alopecia is one type of alopecia which affects 40 million men and 20 million women in the United States.

    A.   When it occurs in males it is often referred to as Male Pattern Baldness.

        1.   It impacts 70% of all men.

        2.   According to the National Alopecia Areata Foundation website that I accessed in March of 2014, it is genetically linked since it is passed down from father to son.

        3.   It begins with an M–shape across the hairline.

    B.   When it occurs in females it is often referred to as Female Pattern Baldness.

        1.   It impacts 40% of all women.

        2.   Females normally lose hair from the top of the scalp.

        3.   It is also genetically linked since it is passed down from mother to daughter.

    C.   Both Male Pattern Baldness and Female Pattern Baldness can begin early in life when the male or female is in his/her teens.

    D.   This type of alopecia rarely leads to total hair loss.

Transition: Now that you know what Androgenetic Alopecia is, let's move on to another type of alopecia.

II. Alopecia Areata, the second type of alopecia, affects millions in the United States.

    A.   According to Alopecia Areata Registry on the University of Texas website document, "MD Anderson Cancer Center" that I accessed March 2014, Alopecia Areata affects 2% of people in the United States.

        1.   It usually presents itself with hair loss in patches, varying in size from 1 cm to relatively large areas.

        2.   According to Madeline Duvic, MD, Chief of Dermatology at MD Anderson's Melanoma and Cancer Center, "Alopecia Areata affects anyone regardless of age, gender or ethnicity."

        3.   Individuals may experience spontaneous remission, but one can also have repeated episodes.

    B.   It is not health damaging, but as with all forms of alopecia, it can affect self-esteem.

        1.   Women often experience psychological distress with the hair loss because our society links femininity and sexuality to hair.

        2.   According to the July 2012 Journal of Health Psychology article "Bald is Beautiful" by Patricia Tucker, hair is often linked to identity and can be the cause of depression.

Transition: Now that you know about Alopecia Areata, let's move on to the third type. Alopecia Universalis.

III. Alopecia Universalis is a type that affects the hair over the entire body.

    A.   According to Heather Brannon's November 2013 article, "Alopecia Areata-Bald Spot" that I found on the About Health website, approximately 60% of the people that have alopecia have this type.

        1.   It usually presents itself before the age of 20.

        2.   This is the type I have had for over 26 years.

        3.   This type of alopecia can affect anyone, at any time.

    B.   The distinction between this type of alopecia and others is that this type affects eyebrows, lashes, nose hairs, and all other body hair.

    C.   Aother distinction is that it also affects fingernails and toenails.

        1.   Normal healthy fingernails and toenails do not break easily and also can be painted.

        2.   Fingernails and toenails of someone with this type of alopecia cannot be painted because that will cause the nail to suffocate and crack all the way down the middle.

CONCLUSION

I.   To conclude, there are three major types of alopecia: Andogenetic Alopecia, Alopecia Areata, and Alopecia Universalis.

II.   As I said earlier, I was not diagnosed until I was 6 years old. That is when I was first taken to the doctor, and he took a piece of hair and sent it off for testing. Soon all my hair started to fall out. In kindergarten, I had just bald spots. In high school, we moved from Corpus to Houston. That is when I lost all my hair. From that point on, I felt the need to conform to the standards of beauty that is thrust upon us all. I wore wigs for years, keeping my Alopecia hidden. In 2009, I removed my wig for the first time when, as a member of a church group, we were all asked to reveal something we usually have kept hidden from others. I took off my wig and held up this sign. (VISUAL: Hold up sign that says "I AM BALD AND I AM LOVED.") I finally realized that I am beautiful, and I have never worn a wig since. You may have heard the saying that beauty is only skin deep. What I have learned is that beauty can also be hair optional.

VISUAL AIDS

PowerPoint pictures of hair follicle, male pattern baldness, alopecia, Alopecia Areata, Alopecia Universalis, nails, and my actual sign.

WORKS CITED

Brannon, Heather. "Alopecia Areata-Bald spot." About.com Health. n.p., 05 Nov 2013. Web. 15 Mar 2014.

"MD Anderson Cancer Center." Alopecia Areata Registry. University of Texas, n.d. Web. 15 Mar 2014.

"National Alopecia Areata Foundation." National Alopecia Areata Foundation. naaf.org, n.d. Web. 15 Mar 2014.

Tucker, Patricia. "Bald is Beautiful—The Psychological Impact of Alopecia Areata." *The Journal of Health Psychology.* July 2012.

This outline was created by Amanda Lea Moya for her informative speech which she delivered in her SPCH 1315 class at Del Mar College. Amanda is a cosmetology major.

Guide for Informative Preparation Outline (Format #2)

I. **Introduction**

   A. **Attention Getter:**
(Question, story, statistic, arousal of curiosity, or other type)

   B. **Establish Credibility:**
(How are YOU linked to this topic?)

   C. **Link to Audience:**
(any subpoints/quotes)

      1. Statistic from class survey

      2. "So, what?"

   D. **Thesis Statement:**
(Preview—LIST—three main points)

II. **Body**

   A. (Write your first main point here)

      1. (any subpoints/quotes)

      2. (any subpoints/quotes)

————————transition written out in full————

   B. (Write your second main point here)

      1. (any subpoints/quotes)

      2. (any subpoints/quotes)

————————transition written out in full————

C.   (Write your third main point here)

    1.   (any subpoints/quotes)

    2.   (any subpoints/quotes)

III. **Conclusion**

A.   **Review Points:**
(Review—LIST—three main points)

B.   **Bow-Tie/Clincher:**
(Match attention-getter)

Bibliography: (In correct APA format)

Example of Informative Outline (Format #2)

Michael Jackson

I. Introduction

    A. Attention Getter—At the age of 2 my son began to listen to Michael Jackson . . .

    B. Establish credibility—I found myself listening to his music . . . That is why I chose this topic.

    C. Link to audience—Although all in the class know who Michael Jackson is, only 25% of you know when his career got started. 75% do not know when it all began.

    D. Thesis—Today I will take you in the path of when it all started as a child, when it transitioned into his adult career and his tragic death.

II. Body

    A. Childhood

        1. He was born in Gary, Indiana, on Aug. 29, 1958. Started his music career at the age of 5 in the group "Jackson 5" which was started by his father. (Funk & Wagnalls New World, 2014)

        2. The Jackson 5 was signed by Motown Entertainment Empire in the late 1960s. (Funk & Wagnalls New World, 2014)

    ———————Now that we know how his career got started, let's talk about how he transitioned into a solo artist as an adult.———————

    B. Adulthood

        1. In the year 1979 at the age of 21, he released the album "Off the Wall" which included the hits "Don't Stop 'til You Get Enough" and "Rock with You." Seven million copies were sold. (Salem Press, 2013)

        2. The album "Thriller" was released in 1982. It included singles like "Billie Jean," "PYT," "Beat It," and "Thriller." (Salem Press, 2013)

            a. Stayed at the top of Billboard's sales charts for 37 weeks.

            b. Sold 110 million copies worldwide.

            c. Earned Jackson eight Grammys including Album of the Year.

            d. He was named the King of Pop.

        3. Other albums followed which included "Bad" and "Dangerous."

    ———————Now that we know how he transitioned into a solo artist as an adult, let's talk about how his life ended.———————

C. Death

    1. In March 2009, Jackson announced his tour "This Is It." (Salem Press, 2013)

    2. On June 25, 2009, just weeks before his tour, Jackson died of cardiac arrest.

    3. In the five years after his death, his estate has earned $700 million, which is more than any other artist dead or alive. (Forbes, 2014)

        a. The film "This Is It" was released.

        b. Ubisoft created a video game.

III. Conclusion

A. Review—Today we have learned more about Michael Jackson's extensive career by talking about his childhood and adulthood career, as well as talking about his tragic death.

B. Clincher—After today, I hope that you are able to see why Michael Jackson was known as the King of Pop, and you are able to enjoy his music as much as my son and I do.

Bibliography

Cullen, J. (2013). 'Thriller' marks Jackson's musical coming-of-age. *Salem Press Encyclopedia*. Retrieved from Research Starters.

How Michael Jackson earned over $700 million since his death. (2014). *Forbes.com*.

Michael Jackson. (2014). *Funk & Wagnalls New World Encyclopedia*, 1(1). Retrieved from EBSCO.

Miller, K. (2013). Michael Jackson. *Salem Press Biographical Encyclopedia*. Retrieved from EBSCO.

Warwick, J. (2012). You can't win, child, but you can't get out of the game. Michael Jackson's transition from child star to superstar. *Popular Music & Society, 35*(2), 241–259. doi.10.1080/03007766.2011.618052

Adriana Mayen, a Speech major at Del Mar College, wrote this outline in preparation for her informative speech in her SPCH 1315 class.

Persuasive Speaking

Key Concepts of Basic Persuasion Theory

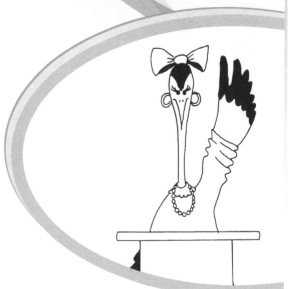

Three Purposes of Persuasive Speaking—shaping responses, reinforcing responses, changing responses

What Is being Influenced? beliefs, values, attitudes, behavior

Principles of Persuasion

consistency persuade—You are more likely to be persuaded if the suggested change is consistent with your beliefs, values, attitudes, and/or behavior.

small change persuade—You are more likely to be persuaded if the suggested change asks for a small change rather than a large change in your ideas or behaviors.

benefits persuade—You are more likely to be persuaded if the benefits of the suggested change outweigh the cost.

fulfilling needs persuade—You are more likely to be persuaded if the suggested change fills some need in your life.

gradual approach persuade—You are more likely to be persuaded if you are persuaded gradually instead of "too much too soon."

Maslow's Hierarchy of Needs

self-actualization needs

esteem needs

belonging needs

safety needs

physiological needs

Persuasive Speech Topics

The following persuasive speech subjects are ones that have been used by former Del Mar students. You can use them to spark your interest in a particular topic for further research for your speech. However, students are almost always more successful when they choose a topic that genuinely interests them. In selecting a persuasive speech topic, consider completing these statements, "It really makes me angry that …" or "Everyone ought to …" Your speech then needs to answer the question "Why?"

- Don't spank your children
- Video games do (do not) promote violence
- Parents should (should not) be able to choose the gender of their child
- All jobs should require mandatory drug testing
- Become a vegetarian
- Humans should (should not) be cloned
- U.S.A. should stop immigration from countries known to harbor terrorists
- Adoptees should have the legal right to find out who their birth parents are
- Large vehicles use too much natural energy—don't buy them
- All U.S. tourists who travel abroad should be legally required to receive appropriate immunizations
- All states should require motorcyclists to wear helmets
- Mothers should (should not) breastfeed in public
- Epileptics should (should not) be allowed to drive
- The legal drinking age should be lowered to eighteen
- Global warming is real/not real
- All parents should take a course in parenting

- Vaccinations should (should not) be compulsory for children
- Juvenile offenders should be tried as adults
- Sea mammals should not be trained for the public's amusement
- Catholic priests should be allowed to marry
- All Hispanics should learn how to speak Spanish
- U.S. companies should hire American employees and stop outsourcing
- Put prayer back in public school
- Don't eat dairy products
- Consumer tax should take the place of income tax
- Student evaluations should have more impact on a teacher's continued employment
- Medical marijuana should be legal in all states
- Welfare recipients should be drug free to qualify for food stamps
- "No Pass/No Play" should be discontinued in Texas
- There should be a ban on owning and breeding pit bulls
- A student's progress should not be determined by standardized tests

Possible Organizations for the "Non-Profit" Persuasive Speech

One option for your persuasive speech is to choose a non-profit organization or cause and to convince your audience to contribute time, talent, service, and/or money to that organization or cause. Below is a sample list of non-profit community and worldwide organizations. Remember that many non-profit organizations are not as visible to the public as some of these listed below, but they still may be a perfect choice. You will notify your instructor which organization/cause you have chosen by completing the Persuasive Topic Declaration in this activity book. After receiving topic approval from your instructor, your objective will be to research, organize, and deliver a persuasive speech convincing your audience to contribute their time, talent, service and/or money to your non-profit organization/cause. All speeches will be organized using Monroe's Motivated Sequence.

- American Cancer Society
- American Red Cross
- Area Agency on Aging of the Coastal Bend
- Big Brothers/Big Sisters of South Texas
- Birthright Counseling
- Charlie's Place
- Coastal Bend Wellness Foundation
- Coastal Bend Blood Center
- Coastal Bend Council on Alcohol and Drug Abuse
- Corpus Christi Animal Rights Efforts (CCARE)
- Corpus Christi Boys and Girls Club
- Corpus Christi Literacy Council
- Corpus Christi Women's Shelter
- Crime Victim Services (A Division of Family Counseling Service)
- Del Mar College Foundation
- Driscoll Children's Hospital
- Family Outreach Corpus Christi, Inc.
- Food Bank of Corpus Christi
- Foster Angels of South Texas Foundation (FAST)
- Friends of the Corpus Christi Museum of Science and History
- Good Samaritan Rescue Mission
- Goodwill Industries of South Texas
- Gulf Coast Council of the Boy Scouts of America
- Gulf Coast Council of the Girl Scouts of America
- Gulf Coast Humane Society
- Harbor Playhouse

- Homeless Issues Partnership
- Juvenile Diabetes Research Foundation
- Locks of Love
- Loving Spoonful
- Lupus Foundation of America
- MADD—Mothers Against Drunk Drivers
- March of Dimes
- Mary McLeod Bethune Day Nursery
- Metro Ministries
- MHMR—Mental Health and Mental Retardation Association of Nueces County
- Muscular Dystrophy Association of Corpus Christi
- National Multiple Sclerosis Society
- Nueces County Child Welfare Foundation
- Nueces County Children's Advocacy Center
- Nueces County Juvenile Justice Volunteers
- Palmer Drug Abuse Program (PDAP)
- Peewee's Pet Adoption and World Sanctuary
- Ronald McDonald House of Corpus Christi
- Salvation Army
- Senior Community Service Employment Program
- Special Olympics
- Saint Jude's Children's Research Hospital
- Southwest Transplant Alliance
- Supply Our Students (SOS—United Way)
- United Way of the Coastal Bend
- USO of South Texas

Speech 1315 Name ______________________________

PERSUASIVE SPEAKING Class Time ______________________________

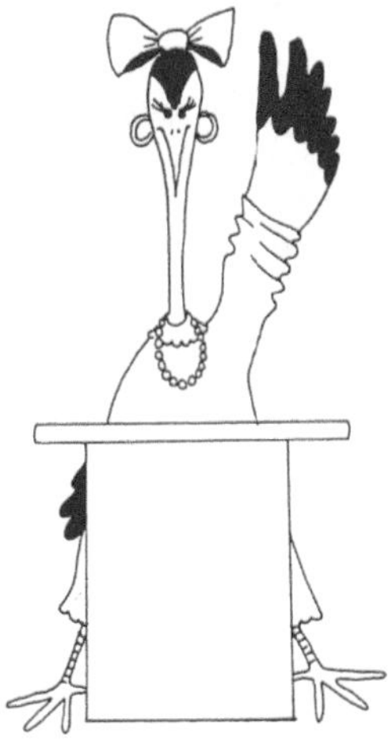

Persuasive Speech Topic Declaration for Monroe's Motivated Sequence: Non-Profit Organization

TOPIC: ______________________________

GENERAL PURPOSE: ______________________________

____

SPECIFIC PURPOSE: ______________________________

____

____

MAIN POINTS:

[1] WRITE A STATEMENT THAT DESCRIBES THE <u>PROBLEM</u> YOUR ORGANIZATION ADDRESSES:

____

____

____

[2] WRITE A STATEMENT THAT DESCRIBES THE <u>SOLUTION</u> YOUR ORGANIZATION OFFERS:

____

____

____

[3]   WRITE A <u>NEGATIVE VISUALIZATION</u>—HOW THE COMMUNITY/PEOPLE WILL BE
      WORSE WITHOUT YOUR ORGANIZATION AND THE SOLUTION(S) IT OFFERS:

_____

_____

_____

      WRITE A <u>POSITIVE VISUALIZATION</u>—HOW THE COMMUNITY/PEOPLE WILL BE
      BETTER WITH YOUR ORGANIZATION AND THE SOLUTION(S) IT OFFERS:

_____

_____

_____

CENTRAL IDEA/THESIS STATEMENT: _____

_____

_____

_____

LIST ONE OR MORE ARGUMENTS THE AUDIENCE MAY HAVE IN OPPOSITION
TO YOUR POSITION (REASONS THEY MIGHT BE HESITANT TO SUPPORT YOUR
ORGANIZATION):

_____

_____

_____

_____

Unless notified by your instructor that your topic is inappropriate or ineffective, this sheet COMMITS you to
this declared topic. You cannot change your topic without approval from your instructor.

Speech 1315 Name *Example*

PERSUASIVE SPEAKING Class Time ____________

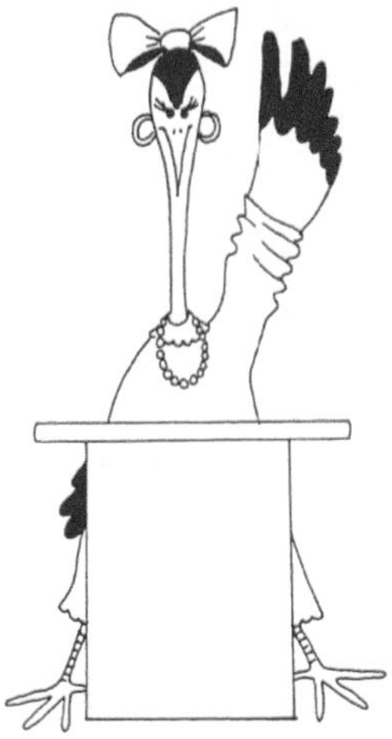

Persuasive Speech Topic Declaration for Monroe's Motivated Sequence: Non-Profit Organization

TOPIC: *Metro Ministries*

GENERAL PURPOSE: *To persuade*

SPECIFIC PURPOSE: *At the end of my speech, the audience will agree to donate the class funds to Metro Ministries.*

MAIN POINTS:

[1] **WRITE A STATEMENT THAT DESCRIBES THE <u>PROBLEM</u> YOUR ORGANIZATION ADDRESSES:**

The homeless in our community experience numerous problems including lack of health care, food, and shelter.

[2] **WRITE A STATEMENT THAT DESCRIBES THE <u>SOLUTION</u> YOUR ORGANIZATION OFFERS:**

Metro Ministries is meeting the needs of the homeless in our community.

[3] WRITE A <u>NEGATIVE VISUALIZATION</u>—HOW THE COMMUNITY/PEOPLE WILL BE WORSE WITHOUT YOUR ORGANIZATION AND THE SOLUTION(S) IT OFFERS:

There will be more homeless individuals trapped in a life where their basic survival needs remain unmet.

WRITE A <u>POSITIVE VISUALIZATION</u>—HOW THE COMMUNITY/PEOPLE WILL BE BETTER WITH YOUR ORGANIZATION AND THE SOLUTION(S) IT OFFERS:

More homeless individuals will have their needs met which gives them the opportunity to become productive members of our community.

CENTRAL IDEA/THESIS STATEMENT: *Metro Ministries is meeting the needs of the homeless in our community, but in order to continue their mission, we all need to commit ourselves to help them achieve their goals by donating our class money to fund their programs.*

LIST ONE OR MORE ARGUMENTS THE AUDIENCE MAY HAVE IN OPPOSITION TO YOUR POSITION (REASONS THEY MIGHT BE HESITANT TO SUPPORT YOUR ORGANIZATION):

1. *The homeless are just looking for a handout.*
2. *I work, so why can't they?*
3. *No one should expect others to take care of them.*
4. *The problem is so large that it is hard to believe anything I do or give will make any real difference.*

Unless notified by your instructor that your topic is inappropriate or ineffective, this sheet COMMITS you to this declared topic. You cannot change your topic without approval from your instructor.

Name _Example_

Class Time _____

Persuasive Speech Topic Declaration for Monroe's Motivated Sequence: General Topic

TOPIC: _Recycle at Your Curb_

GENERAL PURPOSE: _To persuade_

SPECIFIC PURPOSE: _At the end of my speech, the audience will agree to recycle their aluminum, plastic, and paper goods by using the Corpus Christi curbside recycling program._

MAIN POINTS:

[1] **WRITE A STATEMENT THAT DESCRIBES THE <u>PROBLEM</u>:**

We all use recyclable products but because too many residents don't participate in the cubside program, the Corpus Christi landfill is increasing in size, which causes multiple problems.

[2] **WRITE A STATEMENT THAT DESCRIBES THE <u>SOLUTION</u>:**

Everyone should recycle their aluminum, plastic, and paper goods by participating in the Corpus Christi curbside program.

[3] **WRITE A <u>NEGATIVE VISUALIZATION</u>—HOW THE COMMUNITY/PEOPLE WILL BE WORSE WITHOUT YOUR SOLUTION:**

The landfill will continue to grow in size, reaching its capacity.

WRITE A <u>POSITIVE VISUALIZATION</u>—HOW THE COMMUNITY/PEOPLE WILL BE BETTER WITH YOUR SOLUTION:

Less trash will end up in our landfills and trash will be able to be used again in the manufacture of new products.

CENTRAL IDEA/THESIS STATEMENT: *While numerous problems exist due to the increasing size of the Corpus Christi landfill, these issues can be eliminated if we all commit to recycling aluminum, plastic, and paper goods through the city's curbside recycling program.*

LIST ONE OR MORE ARGUMENTS THE AUDIENCE MAY HAVE IN OPPOSITION TO YOUR POSITION (REASONS THEY MIGHT BE HESITANT TO SUPPORT YOUR ORGANIZATION):

1. *My time is valuable, and this would take too much time.*

2. *I don't have one of the large blue containers for recycling.*

3. *If I don't recycle, it isn't going to make that much of a difference to our landfill.*

Unless notified by your instructor that your topic is inappropriate or ineffective, this sheet COMMITS you to this declared topic. You cannot change your topic without approval from your instructor.

Guide for Persuasive Preparation Outline (Format #1) (Following Monroe's Motivated Sequence)

Use the following guide to develop your preparation outline for your **PERSUASIVE** Speech. This sample guide has three main points in the body of the speech. In your speech, the number and the organization of main points, subpoints, and sub-subpoints will vary depending on the topic and purpose of your speech. However, the elements needed in the outline—title, specific purpose statement, central idea, introduction, body, conclusion, transition statements, visual aids, and bibliography/works cited—will remain the same. **For more information, check your textbook and refer to the Del Mar student's persuasive speech in this activity book.** Write out your introduction and conclusion in its entirety (using Roman numerals I and II to indicate attention getting material and orienting material in your introduction and Roman numeral I and II for the summary statement and the clincher technique in your conclusion). The body of your speech will then indicate main points and subpoints (utilizing Roman numerals for main points and capital letters for subpoints, etc.) with information that is formulated in one full sentence per outline symbol.

Name:_____

Date:_____

Course Time:_____

TITLE
(This should be your speech title.)

General Purpose: To persuade

Specific Purpose: (Should fit the requirements for specific purpose statements—check textbook.)

Central Idea/Thesis Statement: (Should fit the requirements for central ideas—check textbook.)

INTRODUCTION:

I. (Write out your entire speech introduction … but put all of your **"attention getting material"** under Roman Numeral I—be creative—using one or more of the following techniques: tell a hypothetical story or a personal narrative, use a quote, arouse curiosity, use an illustration or an example, present startling information, use a visual aid, or do a demonstration.)

II. (Write out the **"orienting material"** portion of your introduction … and put it all under Roman Numeral II. This portion should include: **your link and/or credibility** toward your speech subject (unless you have used a narrative in your attention getter and then this function may have been already satisfied), **the common ground you have with your audience** (the audience's link to the speech subject—what's in it for them), **background information** (if necessary … defining terms etc.), and the **central idea statement** (this should clearly preview main points of your speech).

BODY:

I. **Main Point: NEED**—A word or phrase that states the main problem or issue that the organization is addressing. (This is not the problem/s that that the organization may be having. The organization should not be even brought up in this first main point.)

   A. **Sub point**—Key word or phrase that identifies one of the specific problems

      1. **Sub-sub point**—This is your supporting material/evidence (examples, illustrations, statistics, testimony, etc.)

      2. **Sub-sub point**—This is your supporting material/evidence (examples, illustrations, statistics, testimony, etc.)

   B. **Sub point**—Key word or phrase that identifies one of the specific problems

      1. **Sub-sub point**—This is your supporting material/evidence (examples, illustrations, statistics, testimony, etc.)

      2. **Sub-sub point**—This is your supporting material/evidence (examples, illustrations, statistics, testimony, etc.)

   C. **Sub point**—Key word or phrase that identifies one of the specific problems

      1. **Sub-sub point**—This is your supporting material/evidence (examples, illustrations, statistics, testimony, etc.)

      2. **Sub-sub point**—This is your supporting material/evidence (examples, illustrations, statistics, testimony, etc.)

Transition: One full sentence that moves the audience from the first main point (NEED) to the second main point (SATISFACTION).

II. **Main Point: SATISFACTION**—A word or phrase that states that the non-profit organization is successfully solving these problems/issues.

    A. **Sub point**—Key word or phrase that identifies one of the ways that the organization is satisfying the problems elaborated in main point I; sub point A.

        1. **Sub-sub point**—This is your supporting material/evidence (example, illustration, statistic, testimony, etc.) Be specific about the program or initiative and the impact that it has had on the problem/issue.)

        2. **Sub-sub point**—This is your supporting material/evidence (example, illustration, statistic, testimony, etc.) Be specific about the program or initiative and the impact that it has had on the problem/issue.)

    B. **Sub point**—Key word or phrase that identifies another way that the organization is satisfying the needs/problems elaborated in main point I; sub point B.

        1. **Sub-sub point**—This is your supporting material/evidence (example, illustration, statistic, testimony, etc.) Be specific about the program or initiative and the impact that it has had on the problem/issue.

        2. **Sub-sub point**—This is your supporting material/evidence (example, illustration, statistic, testimony, etc.) Be specific about the program or initiative and the impact that it has had on the problem/issue.

    C. **Sub point**—Key word or phrase that identifies that some individuals may be hesitant to contribute to this organization.

        1. **Sub-sub point**—Key word or phrase that identifies one of the argument that that audience members might have for not contributing to this organization.

            a. **Sub-sub-sub point**—Key word or phrase that refutes this argument (example, statistic, testimony, etc.)

            b. **Sub-sub-sub point**—Key word or phrase that refutes this argument (example, statistic, testimony, etc.)

        2. **Sub-sub point**—Key word or phrase that identifies another argument that the audience members might have for not contributing to this organization.

            a. **Sub-sub-sub point**—Key word or phrase that refutes this argument.

            b. **Sub-sub-sub point**—Key word or phrase that refutes this argument.

Transition: One full sentence that moves the audience smoothly from main point II (SATISFACTION) to main point III (VISUALIZATION).

III. **Main Point: VISUALIZATION**—Key word or phrase that states that the audience should visualize what our community or world be like if this organization continues its mission and what will occur if they cannot do so.

    A. **Sub point**—Key word or phrase that states how the community/world will be impacted positively if this organization continues to get monetary support.

        1. **Sub-sub point**—Key word or phrase that paints a picture of impact.

        2. **Sub-sub point**—Key word or phrase that paints a picture of impact.

B. **Sub point**—Key word or phrase that states how the community/world will be impacted negatively if this organization fails to be monetarily supported.

    1. **Sub-sub point**—Key word or phrase that paints a picture of impact.

    2. **Sub-sub point**—Key word or phrase that paints a picture of impact.

CONCLUSION:

I. (Your conclusion should be written out word for word as you intend to say it in your speech. Your **summary statement,** which is basically a re-wording of your central idea statement, should be written out under Roman Numeral I.)

II. (Action/Appeal)

VISUAL AID (List separately and identify content)

WORKS CITED (MLA or APA format—check with your instructor's requirement.)

Name _____

Class Time _____

Checklist for Writing a Persuasive Preparation Outline

(Format #1)

Check off the following items that need to be included in your speech outline.

OUTLINE FORMAT

____Title written at top

____General purpose included

____Specific purpose included

    ____begins with "At the end of my speech …"

    ____reference to audience

    ____specific, not general

    ____realistic objectives

____Central idea/thesis statement included

____Consistent form used

    ____complete sentence or keyword

    ____transitions (between main points)

    ____subdivisions (minimum of two—every "A" needs a "B"; every "1" needs "2," etc.)

INTRODUCTION

____Attention material included

    ____grabs listener's interest

____Orienting material included

    ____prepares the audience for the body of the speech

    ____includes speaker credibility/link to topic

    ____includes audience link to topic

    ____previews the speech's main points

    ____state speaker's position on issue

BODY

____Main points included

    ____have the appropriate number of main points

    ____support the specific purpose

    ____organized effectively

____Support materials included

    ____uses different types of support materials

    ____contains adaquate support information

    ____includes sufficient evidence to support your position on the issue

CONCLUSION

____"Brakelight" included (signal the end)

____Summary of main points included

____Avoids introducing new information

    ____Includes clincher

____Ends with appeal to audience about issue

WORKS CITED

____Minimum of three sources included

____Proper MLA or APA form (check with instructor for his/her requirement)

VISUAL AID(S)

____Each listed separately (identifying content)

Example of Persuasive Outline (Format #1)

Foster Youth Life Investment Partners

General Purpose: To persuade

Specific Purpose: At the end of my speech, the audience will agree to donate the class funds to the Foster Youth Life Investment Partners Organization.

Central Idea: The Foster Youth Life Investment Partners are addressing extensive problems associated with individuals who age out of the foster care system, and they deserve our monetary support to continue their mission.

INTRODUCTION

I. Imagine turning 18, right out of high school, and being told you no longer have a place to call home. You graduate from high school, you think you have it all figured out, and you register for college classes thinking school is going to be your only worry. But then you find out that you now have to figure out where you will be laying your head every night and if you are going to have a bed to sleep in. This situation is the reality for a majority of foster children who are too old for continued state-funded care.

II. Not all foster children are lucky enough to have foster parents like mine who were happy to let me and my foster brothers and sisters stay with them while we make the transition into becoming adults. According to my class survey, the majority of you have or had someone you could count on when graduating from high school whether it be a mom, dad, aunt, uncle, brother, or sister. Only four of you indicated that you live completely independent (living on your own), paying your own rent and other living expenses. We know that it is hard for anyone, but it is next to impossible for some foster kids because they don't know where to turn for the help they need. The Foster Youth Investment Partners is a non-profit organization that is addressing the needs of foster children who have aged out of the system, and they deserve our monetary support to help them continue their mission.

BODY

I. Our community is faced with extensive problems associated with foster youth who are aging out of the foster care system.

    A. One of the problems that children who have aged out of the foster care system is that they don't have a home.

        1. According to the "HUD Report Explores Options for Youth Aging Out of Foster Care," an article on the National Alliance to End Homelessness website written by Mindy Mitchell and last updated June 2, 2014, there are more than 70,000 youth in foster care ranging in age between 16 and 20.

2. Every year some 28,000 of those youth age out of the system with very few resources to help them transition into economically independent adulthood.

3. Between 11 and 37 percent of youth aging out of foster care experience homelessness after they transition.

4. To rent an apartment, even a studio, costs on the average of $550–$650 a month in Corpus Christi.

    a. To sign a lease without full-time employment and no previous credit is impossible without a suitable co-signer.

    b. A deposit is also required that can equal as much as one to one and a half times the monthly rent.

B. For all of these reasons, 25 to 50 percent of older foster youth are unstably housed by living with friends, usually just moving from one house to the next after outstaying their welcome.

C. According to the Foster Youth Investment Program website, which I accessed on July 14, 2014, a community assessment was conducted in Corpus Christi to determine available local services and gaps in services to transitioning foster youth.

1. The report found that they do not have a way for their basic survival needs to be met.

2. They don't have money for food, so they often go hungry.

3. They lack money for transportation, which hinders their ability to get and keep a job.

4. They cannot meet their medical needs.

D. Another problem that foster kids who age out of the system deal with is the lack of life skills.

1. Kenia Dimas, the President of the FYLIP organization, informed me in a phone interview on July 31, 2014, that the foster youth struggle with everyday tasks due to the lack of life skills.

2. Many foster youth have no one to teach them the basics about what it takes to succeed in the real world.

    a. They don't know how to budget money.

    b. They don't know how to open a bank account.

    c. They don't know how to acquire electricity, water, cable, etc.

Transition: Now that you realize the problems that foster youth that age out of the system face, let's move on to just what the FYLIP organization is doing to help resolve these issues.

II. The problem of homelessness for the foster youth who age out of the system is being addressed by FYLIP.

A. The FYLIP organization is providing all that they can to ensure that there are fewer homeless foster youth when they leave foster care.

1. They provide youth with the resources needed to get into the housing program.

2. They provide help by paying the deposit on an apartment for the youth.

3. They also assist by providing loans if needed.

B. The FYLIP organization is faced with trying to help the youth with the basic essentials to maintain a stable home environment.

    1. They have a donation room where any donations such as shampoo, towels, furniture, etc., are kept so that when anyone is need, they may have these items.

    2. They also help paying utilities if needed so the youth don't have to go without their electric service or water.

C. The organization has to face trying to help the youth with the basic everyday life skills needed to function.

    1. They help them by providing a support group which is held on the 1st and 3rd Wednesday of every month where they talk about different issues they are facing and find out the needs of the youth.

        a. They help them file their taxes.

        b. They provide help with filling out an application for a job.

    2. They provide cooking classes so that the youth may learn how to prepare appropriate meals for themselves, starting with learning how to make a grocery list.

    3. They financially assist with getting school supplies and textbooks.

D. I know some of you may be thinking to yourself, "Why should I care?"

    1. Someone you know or love could be in the same situation, and you would hope that they would get the help they need.

    2. You may be thinking that money donated will be used to pay the staff or employees of the organization, but all the people involved with FYLIP are volunteers so the funds go directly to help make a difference in the future of foster youth.

Transition: Now, let's examine how our community will be impacted if this organization has the opportunity to continue its mission.

III. VISUALIZATION

A. Picture our community if the Foster Youth Life Investment organization continues to receive necessary support and what it will be like if they fail to receive the monetary help they need.

B. Visualize what our community will be like if FYLIP doesn't receive the monetary support necessary to continue their mission.

    1. If nothing is done to continue to help this organization there will be a lot more homeless young people in the community with nowhere to go.

    2. There would be a lot of youth with nothing to look forward to and feeling like they are worthless, and they will continue to believe that no one cares.

C. Let's imagine that the Foster Youth Life Investment Partners organization continues to receive the necessary support it needs to meet their goals.

    1. There would be fewer homeless youth in the area.

    2. There would be more successful youth because they will have the support they need in order to succeed in life.

CONCLUSION

I.   In closing, the Foster Youth Life Investment Partner organization is a nonprofit organization that is made up of volunteers who help youth transition into adulthood. This could be scary for some, especially when they wake up one morning to be told they have to leave, with no one to count on for support in making this transition.

II. I urge you to vote to give our class funds to help support foster care youth who are not as lucky as you or I. Don't let them feel alone with no support. Give them the opportunity to become a productive member of our society. Let them know that someone does care and that they are not forgotten.

WORKS CITED

Dimas, Kenia. President of Foster Youth Life Investment Partners Organization. Phone Interview. July 31, 2014.

Foster Youth Life Investment Partners. "The Need is Real." 2014. n.p. Web. 31 July 2014.
< http://www.fylip.org/index.html >

Mitchelle, Mindy. "HUD Report Explores Options for Youth Aging out of Foster Care." National Alliance to End Homelessness. 2 June 2014. Web. 8 Aug. 2014.

This outline was created by Del Mar student, Vivian Escochea, in preparation for her persuasive speech in her SPCH 1315 class. Vivian is a Radiological Technician major.

Guide for Persuasive Preparation Outline (Format #2) Following Monroe's Motivated Sequence

General Purpose: _____

Specific Purpose: _____

_____

Central Idea/Thesis: *Today I will convince you there are problems associated with* _____, *explain how (organization) is addressing these problems and persuade you to help this organization continue their mission.*

I. **Introduction (Attention-Step)**

    A. **Attention-Getter:** (story, rhetorical question, quotation, arousal of curiosity, startling statistic, etc.)

    B. **Establish Credibility:** (Why did you choose this topic?)

    C. **Link to Audience:**

        1. Results of classroom survey, statistics, etc.

        2. So, what?

    D. **Central Idea/Thesis:** (copied from above)

II. **Body**

    A. **Need/Problem Step**

        1. **Statement of the problem (clear and concise)**
          "The problem is … ." (this is what your organization helps to "fix")

        2. **Describe the problem/s** (use stories, statistics, examples, etc.)

        3. **Point the problem/s to the audience:** (why is this a problem to the audience)

(Transition)

B. **Satisfaction/Solution Step**

   1. **Statement of the solution (clear and concise)**
       "These problems are being addressed by (organization) ."

   2. **Explanation of the solution**
       (Tell how your organization addresses the problems listed in section "A".)

   3. **Overcome Possible Objections**
       (Bring up arguments against your solution and counter them.)
       "Some of you may be thinking _____, however, _____."

(Transition)

C. **Visualization Step**

   1. *"Picture a world without (your organization)."*
       Describe the bad things that will happen without the financial support for your organization.

   2. *"Picture a world with the help of (your organization)."*
       Describe how much better things would be.

III. **Conclusion (Action Step)**

   A. **Summarize Body of Speech**

   B. **Call audience to Action**
       (Ask audience to vote to give the donation to your non-profit organization.)

   C. **Contact Information** (phone # and/or web address)

   D. **Bow-tie/Clincher**

Bibliography
(In correct APA form)

Name _____

Class Time _____

Example of Persuasive Outline (Format #2) Following Monroe's Motivated Sequence

Coastal Bend Small Breed Rescue

I. **Introduction (Attention-Step)**

   A. **Attention-Getter:**
      Every time there is extreme weather, my mom tells me . . .

   B. **Establish Credibility:**
      I picked this topic because I am a huge pet person . . .

   C. **Link to Audience:**

      1. Survey: 75% are pet owners . . .

      2. So, what?: Our pets are family to us, so almost all of us have a special place in our hearts for pets in general . . .

   D. **Central Idea/Thesis Statement:**
      Today I will convince you of the problems associated with pet overpopulation, explain how the Coastal Bend Small Breed Rescue is addressing these problems, and persuade you to help this organization continue their mission.

II. **Body**

   A. **Need/Problem Step**

      1. **Statement of the problem:**
         The problem is Corpus Christi has a pet overpopulation problem.

      2. **Describe the problem:**

         a. Pet Overpopulation
            (Pet overpopulation is a problem in the United States that still ranks as the number 1 killer of dogs and cats . . . *DVM: The Newsmagazine of Veterinary Medicine,* July 2011)

         b. Euthanasia
            (Approximately 6 to 8 million dogs and cats enter shelters across the country each year; 3 to 4 million of those animals are euthanized in the shelter system . . . *Albany Law Review,* 2011)

      3. **Point the problem/s to the audience:**

         a. We don't like seeing stray animals run around throughout our city.

         b. We need to stop saying "Aww" and start doing something about this problem.

Transition: Now that you know how big the problem is, let's move on to see how the Coastal Bend Small Breed Rescue is helping this problem.

    B. **Satisfaction/Solution Step**

        1. **Statement of the solution:**
            The Coastal Bend Small Breed Rescue is providing a solution by taking in these homeless animals and providing them shelter until they have a new home.

        2. **Explanation of the solution:** (www.cbrescue.webege.com, Dec 2014)

            a. Who do they rescue?

                1. Rescue small animals up to 20 pounds

                2. From owners no longer wanting a pet, strays from the streets, and sometimes from the pound

            b. What do they provide?

                1. Spay and Neuter

                2. Vaccinations

                3. Heart worm prevention

                4. Flea and tick prevention

                5. Collar and Leash

                6. DVD training and pet food coupons

                7. Most pets are micro-chipped

        3. **Overcoming Possible Objections**

            a. Don't know where the money goes

                1. Spay and neutering

                2. None to administration

            b. Don't have the money

                1. Donate time

                2. Spread information to someone interested

Transition: Now that we know what the Coastal Bend Small Breed Rescue is doing to fix the problem, let's see what will happen if they don't receive enough financial support and what will happen if they do.

    C. **Visualization Step**

        1. ***"Picture a world without the Coastal Bend Small Breed Rescue"***

            a. No spay or neutering

            b. No helping out animals or educating people who adopt

        1. ***"Picture a world with the help of the Coastal Bend Small Breed Rescue"***

            c. Continue taking animals in

            d. Continue spaying and neutering

            e. Continue helping those out who adopt

III. **ConclusioN**

    A. **Summarize Body of Speech:**

        You now know the problem with pet overpopulation in Corpus Christi, and how the Coastal Bend Small Breed Rescue helps with fixing this problem. Without the Coastal Bend Small Breed Rescue these homeless animals would have nowhere to go and have no hope for a future.

    B. **Call to Action:**

        We need to work together to fix the pet overpopulation issue in Corpus Christi. The money this class has put together will go straight to the animals and help spay and neuter them which will cut down on the number of unwanted pets. This will help the Coastal Bend Small Breed Rescue continue their dream in helping animals find a new home and provide them a roof over their heads. Please, vote to donate to the Coastal Bend Small Breed Rescue.

    C. **Contact Information:**

        For more information contact them at 361-939-9462, go to their website at www.cbrescue. webege.com, or visit their Facebook page.

    D. **Bow-Tie/Clincher:**

        Next time you see stray animals, now you know of another no-kill shelter that is trying their best to improve the lives of pets and the Corpus Christi community.

Bibliography

Coastal Bend Small Breed Rescue. (Dec 2014). Home. Retrieved from http://www.cbrescue.webege.com

Fellenstein, S. (2011, July). New York City veterinarian takes on pet overpopulation. *DVM: The Newsmagazine of Veterinary Medicine, 42,* (7), 43–44. Retrieved May 2, 2015 from Ebsco.

Kenny, K. (2011). A local approach to a national problem: Local ordinances as a means of curbing puppy mill production and pet overpopulation. *Albany Law Review, 75,* (1), 379–406. Retrieved May 2, 2015 from Ebsco.

Patterson, L. (2007, August). Redemption: The myth of pet overpopulation and the No Kill Revolution in America. *Library Journal, 132,* (13), 109. Retrieved May 2, 2015 from Ebsco.

This outline was prepared by Liana Martinez for a speech given in her SPCH 1315 class at Del Mar College. Liana is majoring in Surgical Technology.

Additional Speaking Experiences

Giving a Toast

Top tips for making the toast:

[1] Do your homework

- Research your audience
- Learn the appropriate dress code for the event

[2] Construct the toast

- Match the tone of your toast to the event
- Use your own words
- Keep your toast brief
- Be complimentary during the entire toast. Avoid embarrassing or crude remarks.
- Exclude inside jokes that only the honoree or a few attendees would find amusing.

[3] Practice, practice, practice

- Practice your toast several times

[4] Gain everyone's attention

- Stand up and use eye contact to quiet your audience and get their attention
- Ask out loud for their attention if necessary

[5] Hold yourself confidently

- Stand up
- Hold your glass in one hand
- Keep your body open

[6] Make eye contact

- Look at the honoree
- Look across the audience

[7] Speak slowly and deliberately

- Breathe
- Use short pauses to calm down
- Speak slowly

[8] Sip from your glass

- Lift your glass and ask everyone to join you
- Sip, not chug, from your glass

Construction of the toast:

[I]   The Introduction—Remind the audience of your purpose.

Examples:

- We have come here today to celebrate/honor (person's name) _____ on his/her (event/celebration) _____.
- We are gathered together this afternoon to celebrate/honor _____ on his/her _____.

[II] The Body—These sentences tell us something about the honoree like personality traits, characteristics he/she is known for, etc. (Be very specific. Tell the audience an appropriate story or two. Keep your comments focused on information that relates to the event. If you are toasting a wedding couple, you might tell us a story that illustrates their loving relationship. If you are toasting a mother-to-be, your story could illustrate that she is responsible and caring.)

Examples:

- _____ is the kind of friend who …
- _____ is the person who you would want to have around when …
- You can count on him/her to _____
- I remember when _____
- We used to _____
- If I could think of one word to describe _____, it would be _____ because …

[III] The Conclusion—Wrap up your comments and raise your glass.

Examples:

- Please join me in toasting our friend/our colleague/my daughter (be specific with the relationship) _____.
- And now, raise your glass and help me honor my husband/my colleague/my neighbor, _____, on his/her _____.

Name _____

Class Time _____

Giving a Toast Evaluation

To be filled out by your instructor:

MISSING	POOR	FAIR	GOOD	EXCELLENT
0 pts.	1–3 pts.	4–7 pts.	8–11 pts.	12–14 pts.

Introduction

You got everyone's attention.

You reminded the audience the purpose of the toast. _____ pts.

Organization of Body

You selected at least two relevant things about the honoree. _____ pts.

Supporting Details

You used specific details to support your main points.

You were complimentary. _____ pts.

Conclusion

You wrapped up your comments.

You raised your glass. _____ pts.

Language

You matched the tone of your toast to the event.

You used language that showed class, grace, and style. _____ pts.

Delivery (nonverbal)

You held your glass in one hand and kept your body open.

You looked at the honoree and the audience. _____ pts.

Delivery (voice)

You spoke with an appropriate speaking rate.

You used good volume. _____ pts.

TOTAL POINTS = GRADE _____

The Speech of Personal Experience

Certain occasions require you to speak of a personal experience. We often hear speeches of personal experience at assemblies, business meetings, club gatherings, religious activities, and in other contexts. You have probably heard such a speech from a war veteran, a news correspondent, a great athlete, a business executive, or any other individual who had an interesting experience to share.

The subject of your speech is a personal experience that you perceive as particularly interesting or entertaining. Careful attention must be given to organization so that the content of your speech is fully understood and appreciated. The content of your speech should be more than a mere reflection of your experience; it should bring the experience to life for your listeners. Add interest by including your own personal feelings and reactions; the experiences and impressions of others; the objects that made your experience thrilling, exciting, funny, unbelievable, etc.

Specific Speech Requirements

- Check with your instructor for the time requirement.
- Extemporaneous delivery
- Speech outlined on note cards
- Introduction designed to gain attention and preview speech
- Two or three obvious main points
- Clear transitions
- Conclusion designed to review speech and restimulate interest
- Practice, practice, practice!

When practicing your presentation, ask yourself the following questions:

- Does my speech merely list a series of persons, places, things, and time without telling the significance of what happened to these persons and things? You should vitalize persons and things by describing what happened and by pointing out what makes this incident unusual, exciting, or funny.

- Does my speech offer sufficient details about the experience? For example, if you rescued a drowning person, do not be satisfied to say, "I jumped in and pulled him out." Tell what he was doing, describe his struggles, tell how deep the water was, how far he was from shore, recount your personal fears and feelings as you pulled him toward shore, tell how the current almost took you under, demonstrate the way you grabbed him by the hair, etc.
- Am I comfortable with my preparation for this speech? To prepare for this speech, you must practice until you are comfortable delivering this speech extemporaneously.

Example of The Speech of Personal Experience

The Power of Music

My hands are shaky, my heart-rate is increasing, and I'm trying my hardest to calm my nerves. This is just another occurrence of the stage fright I experience before any concert I've ever played in. One would assume that after playing viola for eight years that I'd be comfortable in performing in front of any crowd, but that is not the case. I get the jitters every single time.

It was my junior year in high school, and several students had been chosen from the Carroll Symphonic Orchestra to play a Christmas concert at the Corpus Christi State School. I was very excited to participate in such a positive event, but I was also nervous at the same time. Most of all, I was anticipating the performance to see if we could make a positive impact on the residents. However, upon entering the state school that day, the atmosphere around me hit me like a brick wall. I almost stopped in my tracks because it felt so depressing and gloomy. I saw hundreds of faces starting back at me and at the stage. Many were unaware of what was happening. I could only feel sorrow because I could only assume that many in the audience had gone through considerable hardships because of their illnesses. On the other hand, I was very excited because hopefully we could change their attitude and make a positive impact on the residents.

That day, we were scheduled to go second after a zesty local German polka band. Obviously, I had to believe that our group would be the less popular of the two. Many people don't enjoy orchestra music. After plenty of clapping and dancing and smiling with the German polka group, the crowd soon settled down.

My doubts soon changed when it was our turn to play. Our first songs were quite a hit. The traditional "We Wish You a Merry Christmas" and "Silent Night" kept the group singing throughout their entirety, but the last song, a jazzed up rendition of "Jingle Bells," won the crowd over. Toward the end of the song, the polka band decided to jump in and join us, so that made much of the crowd start dancing. Even some of the students in our orchestra started singing along as they played their instruments, and one resident of the state school started dancing with our music conductor. After the song ended, I had to say that we received the loudest, most enthusiastic standing ovation our group has ever experienced. The residents really appreciated our music.

This concert was not only a charitable event—it changed my life because it was a great learning experience for me. I think back to it after all these years because our performance truly transformed those residents that day. They went from being really depressed and unaware of what was happening, and our songs gave them a reason to celebrate and be happy. So that day, I truly learned the universal power of music.

This Speech of Personal Experience was delivered by Kathryn Salazar in her public speaking class. Kathryn is a Registered Nursing major at Del Mar College.

What's Your Dream?

Objectives

- To ease some of the speech anxiety felt in the class,
- to briefly (one or two minutes) relate information about yourself and your dream so other classmates will be better acquainted with you.

Instructions

[1] Choose a specific year in the future when you hope to be living your "dream." It could be next year, ten years from now, or in the distant future, but it must be specific (example, 2018 or 2046). Sometime during the speech, tell us how old you will be in that year. In the speech, be very clear how you will be living your dream. You may relate how sticking to your goals helped you achieve your dream. Be clear about what obstacles you overcame and/or what special talents you have and/or what "bumps" in the road might have deferred your dream. *Do not have as your dream that you won the lottery or inherited millions from some unknown relative.* Although that would be nice (!), keep the dream more realistic; what you can achieve with education, perseverance, and determination. Remember to give some thought to your choice. What you share makes a strong impression on your classmates. Your dream should be appropriate for an educational setting.

[2] Jot down your "dream" and what it reveals about who you are and what path your life will take. Be specific about what you do and how you spend your days. Mention the people who are in your life.

[3] Plan your *grabber*. Start your presentation creatively. *Don't say,* "My name is _____ and in 2020 I'll be 30." Say instead, "Ever since the birth of my little sister, Amy, I have wanted to work with other children with Down Syndrome. My whole family loves Amy, and I wanted to extend that love as a teacher for other families with Down Syndrome kids. Here it is 2020, and I have just landed a job with a school in Dallas that specifically educates these special children." To conclude, *don't say,* "That's it, that's all I have to say" or "That's me. I'm done." Every speech must have a *clincher.* That is a creative statement that lets the audience know you are finished.

[4] Read over your notes and decide what you want to share with the class. Remember that you only have one to two minutes to speak! On index cards, write down a few key words and phrases to jog your memory while delivering your speech.

[5] Practice this oral activity point by point (not word for word) until you can deliver the information with only occasional glances at your notes. Know your grabber very well.

[6] When it is your turn to speak, go to the front of the room, pause, and then begin. Look directly at your audience while speaking. Smile. ☺ Glance at your notes just long enough to pick up the cue for your next item. Speak in a natural conversational style, as if you were talking to a group of friends.

[7] After you have finished speaking, pause briefly before you return to your seat.

[8] Remember, **all of your classmates and your professor want you to succeed!**

[9] Check with your professor about his/her specific evaluation criteria for this assignment.

Example of What's Your Dream?

Finding the Cure

I was stunned when I received a call from my mother who was in the emergency room. In this case, it wasn't because of any illness she had, but my aunt had just been diagnosed with cancer.

Ever since that call, my dream goal was to become a doctor and find a cure for cancer. It's now 2022. I've just turned twenty-eight, and I have eleven years of college and medical school behind me. Even with my mom, dad, and brother supporting my efforts both financially and emotionally, I have overcome huge obstacles. Before all the books and studying, time with family and friends seemed like a daily routine. Afterward, socialization decreased to nearly nothing. It was hard not being able to enjoy the fun things in life.

The past two years, I've been working in a lab inside a hospital. A typical day for me is beyond outrageous. I wake up every morning around seven o'clock and get ready for another long day of research. At the lab facility, a detailed routine is followed: research, experiments, collecting data and then doing it all over again. My day usually ends with no final answer for a cure, but I've spend countless hours trying to find the right solution to change the world. On one particular day, all that changed.

One Tuesday afternoon, I believed I found the cure for cancer. With this in mind, I notified another doctor, and we used it on the next patient who needed our help and evaluation. When the results came back for this patient, the cancer was gone as it was for many, many other patients who wanted my treatments.

I am the first person to find a cure for this horrifying disease, the disease we call cancer.

This speech was presented by Armando Perez III, a Del Mar College student with a major in biology.

Speech 1315

SPEECH EVALUATION

Name _____

Class Time _____

"What's Your Dream?" Evaluation

To be filled out by instructor:

<u>MISSING</u>	<u>POOR</u>	<u>FAIR</u>	<u>GOOD</u>	<u>EXCELLENT</u>
0 pts.	1–4 pts.	5–6 pts.	7–8 pts.	9–10 pts.

[1] You began your speech in a creative manner. _____ pts.

[2] You told the audience your age and the year when your dream takes place. _____ pts.

[3] The content of your presentation revealed obstacles you overcame and/or how you spend your days living your dream _____ pts.

[4] You had a clear and creative conclusion. _____ pts.

[5] Your material showed prior thought and preparation. _____ pts.

[6] You presented your dream with enthusiasm/sincerity. _____ pts.

[7] You used good posture and natural gestures. _____ pts.

[8] Your face was expressive. _____ pts.

[9] You looked at the audience most of the time and did not read your speech from your note cards _____ pts.

[10] You adhered to time requirements/restrictions. _____ pts.

TOTAL POINTS = GRADE _____

Comments:

The Impromptu Speech

Impromptu means "spur-of-the-moment" speaking. You use impromptu speaking when you have to give a speech without prior notice. In most situations, you won't be asked to do an impromptu speech unless you have some knowledge about the subject. Impromptu situations occur in meetings, social gatherings, conferences, classrooms, work environments, and similar situations.

Specific Speech Requirements

- Utilize a simple organizational pattern. Whether it be the topical pattern, problem/solution, or another pattern that you can quickly recall, remember to make it simple.
- Start off with a grabber. Do not begin with "I've been asked to speak about …" or "I'm going to tell you about …"
- Preview your topic with a central idea statement. Example: "I think there are two reasons why a student should initially chose a community college over a four-year institution."
- Elaborate on two or three main points.
- End with a review and a clincher. Do not end with "That's it!" or "I guess that's all I have to say," or some other weak ending.

When faced with an impromptu speaking situation, remember the following tips:

- Plan ahead for impromptu situations. Analyze the occasion to see if there is a possibility that you might be asked to speak. For instance, if you are the chair of a committee, you may be called upon at the company meeting.
- Listen carefully to the exact issue you are asked to address. Your comments should relate directly to what is asked. If you genuinely are unfamiliar with the issue, be honest about your knowledge level.
- Remain calm and poised. Even if you do not feel calm and poised because you are surprised at being asked to speak, this is not the time to "fall apart." Remember, your audience wants you to succeed.
- Never apologize for being unprepared. The very nature of impromptu speaking dictates that you are unprepared, so begin your speech with a grabber and not with an apology. End your speech with a clincher and not an apology.

Name _____

Class Time _____

Impromptu Speech Evaluation

To be filled out by your instructor:

<u>MISSING</u>	<u>POOR</u>	<u>FAIR</u>	<u>GOOD</u>	<u>EXCELLENT</u>
0 pts.	1–3 pts.	4–7 pts.	8–11 pts.	12–14 pts.

Introduction

Attention getter _____ pts.

Clear Central Idea

Main points previewed _____ pts.

Organization of Body

Transitions _____ pts.

Supporting Details _____ pts.

Conclusion

Review _____ pts.

Clincher _____ pts.

Delivery

Eye contact _____ pts.

Vocals _____ pts.

Gestures _____ pts.

Spontaneity/Enthusiasm/Sincerity _____ pts.

TOTAL POINTS = GRADE _____

COMMENTS:

Feedback Forms

Your Responsibility as a Speech Critiquer

When someone speaks, the assumption, although sometimes faulty, is that someone else is listening. Listening then, is actually the counterpart of speaking. Certainly in the public speaking process there is no speech without listeners. The listener is one-half of the entire communication process.

In order to fulfill your responsibilities as an audience member in this course, you will be learning and practicing the skill of critical listening. Critical listening means using your abilities and skills to better evaluate the content, organization, language, and delivery of a speaker's presentation.

Since feedback is the primary means by which we learn to improve, especially in the classroom, the specific judgements you make about speech content and delivery need to be presented effectively to the speaker.

For all the above reasons, the remainder of this activity book is comprised of speech evaluation forms. Since these forms give you clear guidelines regarding the criteria for each of your major speeches delivered over this semester, they will facilitate your skill as a critical listener in the classroom. You are provided multiple copies of these Speech Critiques so that each of your fellow classmates can benefit from your feedback.

Commit yourself to becoming the most effective listener you can be. By doing so, you will become a more effective speaker.

Student Feedback on Course

This is an optional course feedback form that you may be asked to respond to anonymously at the end of the semester. If you choose to fill out this form on your own initiative, it will also be welcomed by your instructor and/or the Department of Communications, Languages, and Reading.

In an attempt to maintain quality in SPCH 1315—Public Speaking, your instructor is seeking your help. Please answer the following questions honestly and thoroughly. Thank you for your assistance.

[1]　The things I found to be most helpful about this course were:

[2]　The course would be improved if the following things were done:

[3]　In addition, I would like to tell my instructor:

Speaker's Name _____

Class Time _____

Speech Critique

0 Not Provided	1 Below Expectations	2 Meets Expectations	3 Exceeds Expectations

Speech Content

- Chose interesting and appropriate topic   0 1 2 3
- Had attention-getting introduction   0 1 2 3
- Organized speech clearly   0 1 2 3
- Used details/examples to clarify main ideas   0 1 2 3
- Used appropriate word choice   0 1 2 3
- Concluded effectively   0 1 2 3

Speaker

- Used good eye contact   0 1 2 3
- Sounded conversational   0 1 2 3
- Avoided distracting mannerisms   0 1 2 3
- Used effective gestures   0 1 2 3
- Used enthusiastic/sincere facial expressions   0 1 2 3
- Spoke at ideal rate   0 1 2 3
- Avoided verbal fillers (uh, um, er, okay, right, like, you know)   0 1 2 3

Speaker's Name _____

Class Time _____

Speech Critique

0 Not Provided	1 Below Expectations	2 Meets Expectations	3 Exceeds Expectations

Speech Content

- Chose interesting and appropriate topic   0 1 2 3
- Had attention-getting introduction   0 1 2 3
- Organized speech clearly   0 1 2 3
- Used details/examples to clarify main ideas   0 1 2 3
- Used appropriate word choice   0 1 2 3
- Concluded effectively   0 1 2 3

Speaker

- Used good eye contact   0 1 2 3
- Sounded conversational   0 1 2 3
- Avoided distracting mannerisms   0 1 2 3
- Used effective gestures   0 1 2 3
- Used enthusiastic/sincere facial expressions   0 1 2 3
- Spoke at ideal rate   0 1 2 3
- Avoided verbal fillers (uh, um, er, okay, right, like, you know)   0 1 2 3

Over-All Impressions:

- Adhered to time requirements/restrictions   0   1   2   3
- Used note cards appropriately   0   1   2   3
- Appeared prepared and practiced   0   1   2   3
- Dressed appropriately   0   1   2   3

Comments:

Best aspects of speech (name at least two):

Areas for improvement:

Over-All Impressions:

- Adhered to time requirements/restrictions   0   1   2   3
- Used note cards appropriately   0   1   2   3
- Appeared prepared and practiced   0   1   2   3
- Dressed appropriately   0   1   2   3

Comments:

Best aspects of speech (name at least two):

Areas for improvement:

Speaker's Name _____

Class Time _____

Speech Critique

	0 Not Provided	1 Below Expectations	2 Meets Expectations	3 Exceeds Expectations

Speech Content

	0	1	2	3
Chose interesting and appropriate topic	0	1	2	3
Had attention-getting introduction	0	1	2	3
Organized speech clearly	0	1	2	3
Used details/examples to clarify main ideas	0	1	2	3
Used appropriate word choice	0	1	2	3
Concluded effectively	0	1	2	3

Speaker

	0	1	2	3
Used good eye contact	0	1	2	3
Sounded conversational	0	1	2	3
Avoided distracting mannerisms	0	1	2	3
Used effective gestures	0	1	2	3
Used enthusiastic/sincere facial expressions	0	1	2	3
Spoke at ideal rate	0	1	2	3
Avoided verbal fillers (uh, um, er, okay, right, like, you know)	0	1	2	3

Speaker's Name _____

Class Time _____

Speech Critique

	0 Not Provided	1 Below Expectations	2 Meets Expectations	3 Exceeds Expectations

Speech Content

	0	1	2	3
Chose interesting and appropriate topic	0	1	2	3
Had attention-getting introduction	0	1	2	3
Organized speech clearly	0	1	2	3
Used details/examples to clarify main ideas	0	1	2	3
Used appropriate word choice	0	1	2	3
Concluded effectively	0	1	2	3

Speaker

	0	1	2	3
Used good eye contact	0	1	2	3
Sounded conversational	0	1	2	3
Avoided distracting mannerisms	0	1	2	3
Used effective gestures	0	1	2	3
Used enthusiastic/sincere facial expressions	0	1	2	3
Spoke at ideal rate	0	1	2	3
Avoided verbal fillers (uh, um, er, okay, right, like, you know)	0	1	2	3

Over-All Impressions:

- Adhered to time requirements/restrictions   0   1   2   3
- Used note cards appropriately   0   1   2   3
- Appeared prepared and practiced   0   1   2   3
- Dressed appropriately   0   1   2   3

Comments:

Best aspects of speech (name at least two):

Areas for improvement:

Over-All Impressions:

- Adhered to time requirements/restrictions   0   1   2   3
- Used note cards appropriately   0   1   2   3
- Appeared prepared and practiced   0   1   2   3
- Dressed appropriately   0   1   2   3

Comments:

Best aspects of speech (name at least two):

Areas for improvement:

Speech Critique

Speaker's Name _____

Class Time _____

0 Not Provided	1 Below Expectations	2 Meets Expectations	3 Exceeds Expectations

Speech Content

• Chose interesting and appropriate topic	0	1	2	3
• Had attention-getting introduction	0	1	2	3
• Organized speech clearly	0	1	2	3
• Used details/examples to clarify main ideas	0	1	2	3
• Used appropriate word choice	0	1	2	3
• Concluded effectively	0	1	2	3

Speaker

• Used good eye contact	0	1	2	3
• Sounded conversational	0	1	2	3
• Avoided distracting mannerisms	0	1	2	3
• Used effective gestures	0	1	2	3
• Used enthusiastic/sincere facial expressions	0	1	2	3
• Spoke at ideal rate	0	1	2	3
• Avoided verbal fillers (uh, um, er, okay, right, like, you know)	0	1	2	3

Speech Critique

Speaker's Name _____

Class Time _____

0 Not Provided	1 Below Expectations	2 Meets Expectations	3 Exceeds Expectations

Speech Content

• Chose interesting and appropriate topic	0	1	2	3
• Had attention-getting introduction	0	1	2	3
• Organized speech clearly	0	1	2	3
• Used details/examples to clarify main ideas	0	1	2	3
• Used appropriate word choice	0	1	2	3
• Concluded effectively	0	1	2	3

Speaker

• Used good eye contact	0	1	2	3
• Sounded conversational	0	1	2	3
• Avoided distracting mannerisms	0	1	2	3
• Used effective gestures	0	1	2	3
• Used enthusiastic/sincere facial expressions	0	1	2	3
• Spoke at ideal rate	0	1	2	3
• Avoided verbal fillers (uh, um, er, okay, right, like, you know)	0	1	2	3

Over-All Impressions:

- Adhered to time requirements/restrictions   0   1   2   3
- Used note cards appropriately   0   1   2   3
- Appeared prepared and practiced   0   1   2   3
- Dressed appropriately   0   1   2   3

Comments:

Best aspects of speech (name at least two):

Areas for improvement:

Over-All Impressions:

- Adhered to time requirements/restrictions   0   1   2   3
- Used note cards appropriately   0   1   2   3
- Appeared prepared and practiced   0   1   2   3
- Dressed appropriately   0   1   2   3

Comments:

Best aspects of speech (name at least two):

Areas for improvement:

Speaker's Name _____

Class Time _____

Speech Critique

0 Not Provided	1 Below Expectations	2 Meets Expectations	3 Exceeds Expectations	

Speech Content

	0	1	2	3
Chose interesting and appropriate topic	0	1	2	3
Had attention-getting introduction	0	1	2	3
Organized speech clearly	0	1	2	3
Used details/examples to clarify main ideas	0	1	2	3
Used appropriate word choice	0	1	2	3
Concluded effectively	0	1	2	3

Speaker

	0	1	2	3
Used good eye contact	0	1	2	3
Sounded conversational	0	1	2	3
Avoided distracting mannerisms	0	1	2	3
Used effective gestures	0	1	2	3
Used enthusiastic/sincere facial expressions	0	1	2	3
Spoke at ideal rate	0	1	2	3
Avoided verbal fillers (uh, um, er, okay, right, like, you know)	0	1	2	3

Speaker's Name _____

Class Time _____

Speech Critique

0 Not Provided	1 Below Expectations	2 Meets Expectations	3 Exceeds Expectations	

Speech Content

	0	1	2	3
Chose interesting and appropriate topic	0	1	2	3
Had attention-getting introduction	0	1	2	3
Organized speech clearly	0	1	2	3
Used details/examples to clarify main ideas	0	1	2	3
Used appropriate word choice	0	1	2	3
Concluded effectively	0	1	2	3

Speaker

	0	1	2	3
Used good eye contact	0	1	2	3
Sounded conversational	0	1	2	3
Avoided distracting mannerisms	0	1	2	3
Used effective gestures	0	1	2	3
Used enthusiastic/sincere facial expressions	0	1	2	3
Spoke at ideal rate	0	1	2	3
Avoided verbal fillers (uh, um, er, okay, right, like, you know)	0	1	2	3

Over-All Impressions:

- Adhered to time requirements/restrictions   0   1   2   3
- Used note cards appropriately   0   1   2   3
- Appeared prepared and practiced   0   1   2   3
- Dressed appropriately   0   1   2   3

Comments:

Best aspects of speech (name at least two):

Areas for improvement:

Over-All Impressions:

- Adhered to time requirements/restrictions   0   1   2   3
- Used note cards appropriately   0   1   2   3
- Appeared prepared and practiced   0   1   2   3
- Dressed appropriately   0   1   2   3

Comments:

Best aspects of speech (name at least two):

Areas for improvement:

Speaker's Name _____

Class Time _____

Speech Critique

0 Not Provided	1 Below Expectations	2 Meets Expectations	3 Exceeds Expectations

Speech Content

Chose interesting and appropriate topic	0	1	2	3
Had attention-getting introduction	0	1	2	3
Organized speech clearly	0	1	2	3
Used details/examples to clarify main ideas	0	1	2	3
Used appropriate word choice	0	1	2	3
Concluded effectively	0	1	2	3

Speaker

Used good eye contact	0	1	2	3
Sounded conversational	0	1	2	3
Avoided distracting mannerisms	0	1	2	3
Used effective gestures	0	1	2	3
Used enthusiastic/sincere facial expressions	0	1	2	3
Spoke at ideal rate	0	1	2	3
Avoided verbal fillers (uh, um, er, okay, right, like, you know)	0	1	2	3

Speaker's Name _____

Class Time _____

Speech Critique

0 Not Provided	1 Below Expectations	2 Meets Expectations	3 Exceeds Expectations

Speech Content

Chose interesting and appropriate topic	0	1	2	3
Had attention-getting introduction	0	1	2	3
Organized speech clearly	0	1	2	3
Used details/examples to clarify main ideas	0	1	2	3
Used appropriate word choice	0	1	2	3
Concluded effectively	0	1	2	3

Speaker

Used good eye contact	0	1	2	3
Sounded conversational	0	1	2	3
Avoided distracting mannerisms	0	1	2	3
Used effective gestures	0	1	2	3
Used enthusiastic/sincere facial expressions	0	1	2	3
Spoke at ideal rate	0	1	2	3
Avoided verbal fillers (uh, um, er, okay, right, like, you know)	0	1	2	3

Over-All Impressions:

- Adhered to time requirements/restrictions   0   1   2   3
- Used note cards appropriately   0   1   2   3
- Appeared prepared and practiced   0   1   2   3
- Dressed appropriately   0   1   2   3

Comments:

Best aspects of speech (name at least two):

Areas for improvement:

Over-All Impressions:

- Adhered to time requirements/restrictions   0   1   2   3
- Used note cards appropriately   0   1   2   3
- Appeared prepared and practiced   0   1   2   3
- Dressed appropriately   0   1   2   3

Comments:

Best aspects of speech (name at least two):

Areas for improvement:

Speaker's Name _____

Class Time _____

Speech Critique

	0 Not Provided	1 Below Expectations	2 Meets Expectations	3 Exceeds Expectations

Speech Content

Chose interesting and appropriate topic	0	1	2	3
Had attention-getting introduction	0	1	2	3
Organized speech clearly	0	1	2	3
Used details/examples to clarify main ideas	0	1	2	3
Used appropriate word choice	0	1	2	3
Concluded effectively	0	1	2	3

Speaker

Used good eye contact	0	1	2	3
Sounded conversational	0	1	2	3
Avoided distracting mannerisms	0	1	2	3
Used effective gestures	0	1	2	3
Used enthusiastic/sincere facial expressions	0	1	2	3
Spoke at ideal rate	0	1	2	3
Avoided verbal fillers (uh, um, er, okay, right, like, you know)	0	1	2	3

Speaker's Name _____

Class Time _____

Speech Critique

	0 Not Provided	1 Below Expectations	2 Meets Expectations	3 Exceeds Expectations

Speech Content

Chose interesting and appropriate topic	0	1	2	3
Had attention-getting introduction	0	1	2	3
Organized speech clearly	0	1	2	3
Used details/examples to clarify main ideas	0	1	2	3
Used appropriate word choice	0	1	2	3
Concluded effectively	0	1	2	3

Speaker

Used good eye contact	0	1	2	3
Sounded conversational	0	1	2	3
Avoided distracting mannerisms	0	1	2	3
Used effective gestures	0	1	2	3
Used enthusiastic/sincere facial expressions	0	1	2	3
Spoke at ideal rate	0	1	2	3
Avoided verbal fillers (uh, um, er, okay, right, like, you know)	0	1	2	3

Over-All Impressions:

- Adhered to time requirements/restrictions   0   1   2   3
- Used note cards appropriately   0   1   2   3
- Appeared prepared and practiced   0   1   2   3
- Dressed appropriately   0   1   2   3

Comments:

Best aspects of speech (name at least two):

Areas for improvement:

Over-All Impressions:

- Adhered to time requirements/restrictions   0   1   2   3
- Used note cards appropriately   0   1   2   3
- Appeared prepared and practiced   0   1   2   3
- Dressed appropriately   0   1   2   3

Comments:

Best aspects of speech (name at least two):

Areas for improvement:

Speaker's Name _____

Class Time _____

Speech Critique

	1	2	3	
0	Below	Meets	Exceeds	
Not	Expectations	Expectations	Expectations	
Provided				

Speech Content

	0	1	2	3
• Chose interesting and appropriate topic	0	1	2	3
• Had attention-getting introduction	0	1	2	3
• Organized speech clearly	0	1	2	3
• Used details/examples to clarify main ideas	0	1	2	3
• Used appropriate word choice	0	1	2	3
• Concluded effectively	0	1	2	3

Speaker

	0	1	2	3
• Used good eye contact	0	1	2	3
• Sounded conversational	0	1	2	3
• Avoided distracting mannerisms	0	1	2	3
• Used effective gestures	0	1	2	3
• Used enthusiastic/sincere facial expressions	0	1	2	3
• Spoke at ideal rate	0	1	2	3
• Avoided verbal fillers (uh, um, er, okay, right, like, you know)	0	1	2	3

Speaker's Name _____

Class Time _____

Speech Critique

	1	2	3	
0	Below	Meets	Exceeds	
Not	Expectations	Expectations	Expectations	
Provided				

Speech Content

	0	1	2	3
• Chose interesting and appropriate topic	0	1	2	3
• Had attention-getting introduction	0	1	2	3
• Organized speech clearly	0	1	2	3
• Used details/examples to clarify main ideas	0	1	2	3
• Used appropriate word choice	0	1	2	3
• Concluded effectively	0	1	2	3

Speaker

	0	1	2	3
• Used good eye contact	0	1	2	3
• Sounded conversational	0	1	2	3
• Avoided distracting mannerisms	0	1	2	3
• Used effective gestures	0	1	2	3
• Used enthusiastic/sincere facial expressions	0	1	2	3
• Spoke at ideal rate	0	1	2	3
• Avoided verbal fillers (uh, um, er, okay, right, like, you know)	0	1	2	3

Over-All Impressions:

- Adhered to time requirements/restrictions   0   1   2   3
- Used note cards appropriately   0   1   2   3
- Appeared prepared and practiced   0   1   2   3
- Dressed appropriately   0   1   2   3

Comments:

Best aspects of speech (name at least two):

Areas for improvement:

Over-All Impressions:

- Adhered to time requirements/restrictions   0   1   2   3
- Used note cards appropriately   0   1   2   3
- Appeared prepared and practiced   0   1   2   3
- Dressed appropriately   0   1   2   3

Comments:

Best aspects of speech (name at least two):

Areas for improvement:

Speaker's Name _____

Class Time _____

Speech Critique

	0 Not Provided	1 Below Expectations	2 Meets Expectations	3 Exceeds Expectations

Speech Content

- Chose interesting and appropriate topic — 0 1 2 3
- Had attention-getting introduction — 0 1 2 3
- Organized speech clearly — 0 1 2 3
- Used details/examples to clarify main ideas — 0 1 2 3
- Used appropriate word choice — 0 1 2 3
- Concluded effectively — 0 1 2 3

Speaker

- Used good eye contact — 0 1 2 3
- Sounded conversational — 0 1 2 3
- Avoided distracting mannerisms — 0 1 2 3
- Used effective gestures — 0 1 2 3
- Used enthusiastic/sincere facial expressions — 0 1 2 3
- Spoke at ideal rate — 0 1 2 3
- Avoided verbal fillers (uh, um, er, okay, right, like, you know) — 0 1 2 3

Speaker's Name _____

Class Time _____

Speech Critique

	0 Not Provided	1 Below Expectations	2 Meets Expectations	3 Exceeds Expectations

Speech Content

- Chose interesting and appropriate topic — 0 1 2 3
- Had attention-getting introduction — 0 1 2 3
- Organized speech clearly — 0 1 2 3
- Used details/examples to clarify main ideas — 0 1 2 3
- Used appropriate word choice — 0 1 2 3
- Concluded effectively — 0 1 2 3

Speaker

- Used good eye contact — 0 1 2 3
- Sounded conversational — 0 1 2 3
- Avoided distracting mannerisms — 0 1 2 3
- Used effective gestures — 0 1 2 3
- Used enthusiastic/sincere facial expressions — 0 1 2 3
- Spoke at ideal rate — 0 1 2 3
- Avoided verbal fillers (uh, um, er, okay, right, like, you know) — 0 1 2 3

Over-All Impressions:

- Adhered to time requirements/restrictions   0   1   2   3
- Used note cards appropriately   0   1   2   3
- Appeared prepared and practiced   0   1   2   3
- Dressed appropriately   0   1   2   3

Comments:

Best aspects of speech (name at least two):

Areas for improvement:

Over-All Impressions:

- Adhered to time requirements/restrictions   0   1   2   3
- Used note cards appropriately   0   1   2   3
- Appeared prepared and practiced   0   1   2   3
- Dressed appropriately   0   1   2   3

Comments:

Best aspects of speech (name at least two):

Areas for improvement:

Speaker's Name _____

Class Time _____

Speaker's Name _____

Class Time _____

Speech Critique

0 Not Provided	1 Below Expectations	2 Meets Expectations	3 Exceeds Expectations

Speech Content

	0	1	2	3
Chose interesting and appropriate topic	0	1	2	3
Had attention-getting introduction	0	1	2	3
Organized speech clearly	0	1	2	3
Used details/examples to clarify main ideas	0	1	2	3
Used appropriate word choice	0	1	2	3
Concluded effectively	0	1	2	3

Speaker

	0	1	2	3
Used good eye contact	0	1	2	3
Sounded conversational	0	1	2	3
Avoided distracting mannerisms	0	1	2	3
Used effective gestures	0	1	2	3
Used enthusiastic/sincere facial expressions	0	1	2	3
Spoke at ideal rate	0	1	2	3
Avoided verbal fillers (uh, um, er, okay, right, like, you know)	0	1	2	3

Speech Critique

0 Not Provided	1 Below Expectations	2 Meets Expectations	3 Exceeds Expectations

Speech Content

	0	1	2	3
Chose interesting and appropriate topic	0	1	2	3
Had attention-getting introduction	0	1	2	3
Organized speech clearly	0	1	2	3
Used details/examples to clarify main ideas	0	1	2	3
Used appropriate word choice	0	1	2	3
Concluded effectively	0	1	2	3

Speaker

	0	1	2	3
Used good eye contact	0	1	2	3
Sounded conversational	0	1	2	3
Avoided distracting mannerisms	0	1	2	3
Used effective gestures	0	1	2	3
Used enthusiastic/sincere facial expressions	0	1	2	3
Spoke at ideal rate	0	1	2	3
Avoided verbal fillers (uh, um, er, okay, right, like, you know)	0	1	2	3

Over-All Impressions:

- Adhered to time requirements/restrictions   0   1   2   3
- Used note cards appropriately   0   1   2   3
- Appeared prepared and practiced   0   1   2   3
- Dressed appropriately   0   1   2   3

Comments:

Best aspects of speech (name at least two):

Areas for improvement:

Over-All Impressions:

- Adhered to time requirements/restrictions   0   1   2   3
- Used note cards appropriately   0   1   2   3
- Appeared prepared and practiced   0   1   2   3
- Dressed appropriately   0   1   2   3

Comments:

Best aspects of speech (name at least two):

Areas for improvement:

Speech Critique

Speaker's Name _____

Class Time _____

	0 Not Provided	1 Below Expectations	2 Meets Expectations	3 Exceeds Expectations

Speech Content

- Chose interesting and appropriate topic   0   1   2   3
- Had attention-getting introduction   0   1   2   3
- Organized speech clearly   0   1   2   3
- Used details/examples to clarify main ideas   0   1   2   3
- Used appropriate word choice   0   1   2   3
- Concluded effectively   0   1   2   3

Speaker

- Used good eye contact   0   1   2   3
- Sounded conversational   0   1   2   3
- Avoided distracting mannerisms   0   1   2   3
- Used effective gestures   0   1   2   3
- Used enthusiastic/sincere facial expressions   0   1   2   3
- Spoke at ideal rate   0   1   2   3
- Avoided verbal fillers (uh, um, er, okay, right, like, you know)   0   1   2   3

Speech Critique

Speaker's Name _____

Class Time _____

	0 Not Provided	1 Below Expectations	2 Meets Expectations	3 Exceeds Expectations

Speech Content

- Chose interesting and appropriate topic   0   1   2   3
- Had attention-getting introduction   0   1   2   3
- Organized speech clearly   0   1   2   3
- Used details/examples to clarify main ideas   0   1   2   3
- Used appropriate word choice   0   1   2   3
- Concluded effectively   0   1   2   3

Speaker

- Used good eye contact   0   1   2   3
- Sounded conversational   0   1   2   3
- Avoided distracting mannerisms   0   1   2   3
- Used effective gestures   0   1   2   3
- Used enthusiastic/sincere facial expressions   0   1   2   3
- Spoke at ideal rate   0   1   2   3
- Avoided verbal fillers (uh, um, er, okay, right, like, you know)   0   1   2   3

Over-All Impressions:

- Adhered to time requirements/restrictions   0   1   2   3
- Used note cards appropriately   0   1   2   3
- Appeared prepared and practiced   0   1   2   3
- Dressed appropriately   0   1   2   3

Comments:

Best aspects of speech (name at least two):

Areas for improvement:

Over-All Impressions:

- Adhered to time requirements/restrictions   0   1   2   3
- Used note cards appropriately   0   1   2   3
- Appeared prepared and practiced   0   1   2   3
- Dressed appropriately   0   1   2   3

Comments:

Best aspects of speech (name at least two):

Areas for improvement:

Speech Critique

Item	0 Not Provided	1 Below Expectations	2 Meets Expectations	3 Exceeds Expectations

Speech Content

	0	1	2	3
• Chose interesting and appropriate topic	0	1	2	3
• Had attention-getting introduction	0	1	2	3
• Organized speech clearly	0	1	2	3
• Used details/examples to clarify main ideas	0	1	2	3
• Used appropriate word choice	0	1	2	3
• Concluded effectively	0	1	2	3

Speaker

	0	1	2	3
• Used good eye contact	0	1	2	3
• Sounded conversational	0	1	2	3
• Avoided distracting mannerisms	0	1	2	3
• Used effective gestures	0	1	2	3
• Used enthusiastic/sincere facial expressions	0	1	2	3
• Spoke at ideal rate	0	1	2	3
• Avoided verbal fillers (uh, um, er, okay, right, like, you know)	0	1	2	3

Speaker's Name _____

Class Time _____

Speech Critique

Speech Content

	0	1	2	3
• Chose interesting and appropriate topic	0	1	2	3
• Had attention-getting introduction	0	1	2	3
• Organized speech clearly	0	1	2	3
• Used details/examples to clarify main ideas	0	1	2	3
• Used appropriate word choice	0	1	2	3
• Concluded effectively	0	1	2	3

Speaker

	0	1	2	3
• Used good eye contact	0	1	2	3
• Sounded conversational	0	1	2	3
• Avoided distracting mannerisms	0	1	2	3
• Used effective gestures	0	1	2	3
• Used enthusiastic/sincere facial expressions	0	1	2	3
• Spoke at ideal rate	0	1	2	3
• Avoided verbal fillers (uh, um, er, okay, right, like, you know)	0	1	2	3

Over-All Impressions:

	0	1	2	3
• Adhered to time requirements/restrictions	0	1	2	3
• Used note cards appropriately	0	1	2	3
• Appeared prepared and practiced	0	1	2	3
• Dressed appropriately	0	1	2	3

Comments:

Best aspects of speech (name at least two):

Areas for improvement:

Over-All Impressions:

	0	1	2	3
• Adhered to time requirements/restrictions	0	1	2	3
• Used note cards appropriately	0	1	2	3
• Appeared prepared and practiced	0	1	2	3
• Dressed appropriately	0	1	2	3

Comments:

Best aspects of speech (name at least two):

Areas for improvement:

Speaker's Name _____

Class Time _____

Speech Critique

	0 Not Provided	1 Below Expectations	2 Meets Expectations	3 Exceeds Expectations

Speech Content

- Chose interesting and appropriate topic — 0 1 2 3
- Had attention-getting introduction — 0 1 2 3
- Organized speech clearly — 0 1 2 3
- Used details/examples to clarify main ideas — 0 1 2 3
- Used appropriate word choice — 0 1 2 3
- Concluded effectively — 0 1 2 3

Speaker

- Used good eye contact — 0 1 2 3
- Sounded conversational — 0 1 2 3
- Avoided distracting mannerisms — 0 1 2 3
- Used effective gestures — 0 1 2 3
- Used enthusiastic/sincere facial expressions — 0 1 2 3
- Spoke at ideal rate — 0 1 2 3
- Avoided verbal fillers (uh, um, er, okay, right, like, you know) — 0 1 2 3

Speaker's Name _____

Class Time _____

Speech Critique

	0 Not Provided	1 Below Expectations	2 Meets Expectations	3 Exceeds Expectations

Speech Content

- Chose interesting and appropriate topic — 0 1 2 3
- Had attention-getting introduction — 0 1 2 3
- Organized speech clearly — 0 1 2 3
- Used details/examples to clarify main ideas — 0 1 2 3
- Used appropriate word choice — 0 1 2 3
- Concluded effectively — 0 1 2 3

Speaker

- Used good eye contact — 0 1 2 3
- Sounded conversational — 0 1 2 3
- Avoided distracting mannerisms — 0 1 2 3
- Used effective gestures — 0 1 2 3
- Used enthusiastic/sincere facial expressions — 0 1 2 3
- Spoke at ideal rate — 0 1 2 3
- Avoided verbal fillers (uh, um, er, okay, right, like, you know) — 0 1 2 3

Over-All Impressions:

- Adhered to time requirements/restrictions   0   1   2   3
- Used note cards appropriately   0   1   2   3
- Appeared prepared and practiced   0   1   2   3
- Dressed appropriately   0   1   2   3

Comments:

Best aspects of speech (name at least two):

Areas for improvement:

Over-All Impressions:

- Adhered to time requirements/restrictions   0   1   2   3
- Used note cards appropriately   0   1   2   3
- Appeared prepared and practiced   0   1   2   3
- Dressed appropriately   0   1   2   3

Comments:

Best aspects of speech (name at least two):

Areas for improvement:

Speaker's Name _____

Class Time _____

Informative Speech Critique

0 Not Provided	1 Below Expectations	2 Meets Expectations	3 Exceeds Expectations

Speech Content

Introduction:

	0	1	2	3
Grabbed audience's attention	0	1	2	3
Established credibility/speaker's link	0	1	2	3
Linked audience to topic	0	1	2	3
Previewed main points/central idea	0	1	2	3

Body:

	0	1	2	3
Provided adequate support materials	0	1	2	3
Orally cited appropriate sources (minimum 3)	0	1	2	3
Organized effectively	0	1	2	3
Provided smooth transitions	0	1	2	3

Conclusion:

	0	1	2	3
Had "brakelight" (signaled the end)	0	1	2	3
Reviewed main points/reword central idea	0	1	2	3
Ended with strong clincher	0	1	2	3

Visual Aids:

	0	1	2	3
Relevant to speech	0	1	2	3
Easy to see/read	0	1	2	3
Presented effectively	0	1	2	3
Followed professional guidelines	0	1	2	3

Speaker's Name _____

Class Time _____

Informative Speech Critique

0 Not Provided	1 Below Expectations	2 Meets Expectations	3 Exceeds Expectations

Speech Content

Introduction:

	0	1	2	3
Grabbed audience's attention	0	1	2	3
Established credibility/speaker's link	0	1	2	3
Linked audience to topic	0	1	2	3
Previewed main points/central idea	0	1	2	3

Body:

	0	1	2	3
Provided adequate support materials	0	1	2	3
Orally cited appropriate sources (minimum 3)	0	1	2	3
Organized effectively	0	1	2	3
Provided smooth transitions	0	1	2	3

Conclusion:

	0	1	2	3
Had "brakelight" (signaled the end)	0	1	2	3
Reviewed main points/reword central idea	0	1	2	3
Ended with strong clincher	0	1	2	3

Visual Aids:

	0	1	2	3
Relevant to speech	0	1	2	3
Easy to see/read	0	1	2	3
Presented effectively	0	1	2	3
Followed professional guidelines	0	1	2	3

Speaker

Eye Contact:
- Looked at all parts of audience — 0 1 2 3
- Referred to note cards appropriately — 0 1 2 3

Gestures and Posture:
- Avoided distracting mannerisms — 0 1 2 3
- Used effective gestures — 0 1 2 3
- Used appropriate facial expressions — 0 1 2 3

Voice:
- Spoke at ideal rate — 0 1 2 3
- Avoided awkward pauses — 0 1 2 3
- Sounded energetic/sincere — 0 1 2 3
- Spoke in a conversational tone — 0 1 2 3

Wording:
- Pronounced words correctly — 0 1 2 3
- Used correct grammar — 0 1 2 3
- Used appropriate word choice — 0 1 2 3
- Avoided verbal fillers (uh, um, er, okay, right, all, like, you know) — 0 1 2 3

Over-All Impressions:
- Adhered to time requirements/restrictions — 0 1 2 3
- Appeared prepared and practiced — 0 1 2 3
- Dressed appropriately — 0 1 2 3
- Used extemporaneous delivery style — 0 1 2 3

Comments:

Best aspects of speech (name at least two):

Areas for improvement:

Speaker

Eye Contact:
- Looked at all parts of audience — 0 1 2 3
- Referred to note cards appropriately — 0 1 2 3

Gestures and Posture:
- Avoided distracting mannerisms — 0 1 2 3
- Used effective gestures — 0 1 2 3
- Used appropriate facial expressions — 0 1 2 3

Voice:
- Spoke at ideal rate — 0 1 2 3
- Avoided awkward pauses — 0 1 2 3
- Sounded energetic/sincere — 0 1 2 3
- Spoke in a conversational tone — 0 1 2 3

Wording:
- Pronounced words correctly — 0 1 2 3
- Used correct grammar — 0 1 2 3
- Used appropriate word choice — 0 1 2 3
- Avoided verbal fillers (uh, um, er, okay, right, all, like, you know) — 0 1 2 3

Over-All Impressions:
- Adhered to time requirements/restrictions — 0 1 2 3
- Appeared prepared and practiced — 0 1 2 3
- Dressed appropriately — 0 1 2 3
- Used extemporaneous delivery style — 0 1 2 3

Comments:

Best aspects of speech (name at least two):

Areas for improvement:

Informative Speech Critique

0 Not Provided	1 Below Expectations	2 Meets Expectations	3 Exceeds Expectations

Speech Content

Introduction:

• Grabbed audience's attention	0	1	2 3
• Established credibility/speaker's link	0	1	2 3
• Linked audience to topic	0	1	2 3
• Previewed main points/central idea	0	1	2 3

Body:

• Provided adequate support materials	0	1	2 3
• Orally cited appropriate sources (minimum 3)	0	1	2 3
• Organized effectively	0	1	2 3
• Provided smooth transitions	0	1	2 3

Conclusion:

• Had "brakelight" (signaled the end)	0	1	2 3
• Reviewed main points/reword central idea	0	1	2 3
• Ended with strong clincher	0	1	2 3

Visual Aids:

• Relevant to speech	0	1	2 3
• Easy to see/read	0	1	2 3
• Presented effectively	0	1	2 3
• Followed professional guidelines	0	1	2 3

Speaker's Name

Class Time

Informative Speech Critique

0 Not Provided	1 Below Expectations	2 Meets Expectations	3 Exceeds Expectations

Speech Content

Introduction:

- Grabbed audience's attention — 0 1 2 3
- Established credibility/speaker's link — 0 1 2 3
- Linked audience to topic — 0 1 2 3
- Previewed main points/central idea — 0 1 2 3

Body:

- Provided adequate support materials — 0 1 2 3
- Orally cited appropriate sources (minimum 3) — 0 1 2 3
- Organized effectively — 0 1 2 3
- Provided smooth transitions — 0 1 2 3

Conclusion:

- Had "brakelight" (signaled the end) — 0 1 2 3
- Reviewed main points/reword central idea — 0 1 2 3
- Ended with strong clincher — 0 1 2 3

Visual Aids:

- Relevant to speech — 0 1 2 3
- Easy to see/read — 0 1 2 3
- Presented effectively — 0 1 2 3
- Followed professional guidelines — 0 1 2 3

Speaker

Eye Contact:

• Looked at all parts of audience	0 1	2	3
• Referred to note cards appropriately	0 1	2	3

Gestures and Posture:

• Avoided distracting mannerisms	0 1	2	3
• Used effective gestures	0 1	2	3
• Used appropriate facial expressions	0 1	2	3

Voice:

• Spoke at ideal rate	0 1	2	3
• Avoided awkward pauses	0 1	2	3
• Sounded energetic/sincere	0 1	2	3
• Spoke in a conversational tone	0 1	2	3

Wording:

• Pronounced words correctly	0 1	2	3
• Used correct grammar	0 1	2	3
• Used appropriate word choice	0 1	2	3
• Avoided verbal fillers (uh, um, er, okay, right, all, like, you know)	0 1	2	3

Over-All Impressions:

• Adhered to time requirements/restrictions	0 1	2	3
• Appeared prepared and practiced	0 1	2	3
• Dressed appropriately	0 1	2	3
• Used extemporaneous delivery style	0 1	2	3

Comments:

Best aspects of speech (name at least two):

Areas for improvement:

Speaker

Eye Contact:

• Looked at all parts of audience	0 1	2	3
• Referred to note cards appropriately	0 1	2	3

Gestures and Posture:

• Avoided distracting mannerisms	0 1	2	3
• Used effective gestures	0 1	2	3
• Used appropriate facial expressions	0 1	2	3

Voice:

• Spoke at ideal rate	0 1	2	3
• Avoided awkward pauses	0 1	2	3
• Sounded energetic/sincere	0 1	2	3
• Spoke in a conversational tone	0 1	2	3

Wording:

• Pronounced words correctly	0 1	2	3
• Used correct grammar	0 1	2	3
• Used appropriate word choice	0 1	2	3
• Avoided verbal fillers (uh, um, er, okay, right, all, like, you know)	0 1	2	3

Over-All Impressions:

• Adhered to time requirements/restrictions	0 1	2	3
• Appeared prepared and practiced	0 1	2	3
• Dressed appropriately	0 1	2	3
• Used extemporaneous delivery style	0 1	2	3

Comments:

Best aspects of speech (name at least two):

Areas for improvement:

Speaker's Name _____

Class Time _____

Informative Speech Critique

0 Not Provided	1 Below Expectations	2 Meets Expectations	3 Exceeds Expectations

Speech Content

Introduction:
- Grabbed audience's attention   0 1 2 3
- Established credibility/speaker's link   0 1 2 3
- Linked audience to topic   0 1 2 3
- Previewed main points/central idea   0 1 2 3

Body:
- Provided adequate support materials   0 1 2 3
- Orally cited appropriate sources (minimum 3)   0 1 2 3
- Organized effectively   0 1 2 3
- Provided smooth transitions   0 1 2 3

Conclusion:
- Had "brakelight" (signaled the end)   0 1 2 3
- Reviewed main points/reword central idea   0 1 2 3
- Ended with strong clincher   0 1 2 3

Visual Aids:
- Relevant to speech   0 1 2 3
- Easy to see/read   0 1 2 3
- Presented effectively   0 1 2 3
- Followed professional guidelines   0 1 2 3

Speaker's Name _____

Class Time _____

Informative Speech Critique

0 Not Provided	1 Below Expectations	2 Meets Expectations	3 Exceeds Expectations

Speech Content

Introduction:
- Grabbed audience's attention   0 1 2 3
- Established credibility/speaker's link   0 1 2 3
- Linked audience to topic   0 1 2 3
- Previewed main points/central idea   0 1 2 3

Body:
- Provided adequate support materials   0 1 2 3
- Orally cited appropriate sources (minimum 3)   0 1 2 3
- Organized effectively   0 1 2 3
- Provided smooth transitions   0 1 2 3

Conclusion:
- Had "brakelight" (signaled the end)   0 1 2 3
- Reviewed main points/reword central idea   0 1 2 3
- Ended with strong clincher   0 1 2 3

Visual Aids:
- Relevant to speech   0 1 2 3
- Easy to see/read   0 1 2 3
- Presented effectively   0 1 2 3
- Followed professional guidelines   0 1 2 3

Speaker

Eye Contact:

	0	1	2	3
Looked at all parts of audience	0	1	2	3
Referred to note cards appropriately	0	1	2	3

Gestures and Posture:

	0	1	2	3
Avoided distracting mannerisms	0	1	2	3
Used effective gestures	0	1	2	3
Used appropriate facial expressions	0	1	2	3

Voice:

	0	1	2	3
Spoke at ideal rate	0	1	2	3
Avoided awkward pauses	0	1	2	3
Sounded energetic/sincere	0	1	2	3
Spoke in a conversational tone	0	1	2	3

Wording:

	0	1	2	3
Pronounced words correctly	0	1	2	3
Used correct grammar	0	1	2	3
Used appropriate word choice	0	1	2	3
Avoided verbal fillers (uh, um, er, okay, right, all, like, you know)	0	1	2	3

Over-All Impressions:

	0	1	2	3
Adhered to time requirements/restrictions	0	1	2	3
Appeared prepared and practiced	0	1	2	3
Dressed appropriately	0	1	2	3
Used extemporaneous delivery style	0	1	2	3

Comments:

Best aspects of speech (name at least two):

Areas for improvement:

Speaker

Eye Contact:

	0	1	2	3
Looked at all parts of audience	0	1	2	3
Referred to note cards appropriately	0	1	2	3

Gestures and Posture:

	0	1	2	3
Avoided distracting mannerisms	0	1	2	3
Used effective gestures	0	1	2	3
Used appropriate facial expressions	0	1	2	3

Voice:

	0	1	2	3
Spoke at ideal rate	0	1	2	3
Avoided awkward pauses	0	1	2	3
Sounded energetic/sincere	0	1	2	3
Spoke in a conversational tone	0	1	2	3

Wording:

	0	1	2	3
Pronounced words correctly	0	1	2	3
Used correct grammar	0	1	2	3
Used appropriate word choice	0	1	2	3
Avoided verbal fillers (uh, um, er, okay, right, all, like, you know)	0	1	2	3

Over-All Impressions:

	0	1	2	3
Adhered to time requirements/restrictions	0	1	2	3
Appeared prepared and practiced	0	1	2	3
Dressed appropriately	0	1	2	3
Used extemporaneous delivery style	0	1	2	3

Comments:

Best aspects of speech (name at least two):

Areas for improvement:

Informative Speech Critique

0 Not Provided	1 Below Expectations	2 Meets Expectations	3 Exceeds Expectations

Speech Content

Introduction:

Grabbed audience's attention	0	1	2	3
Established credibility/speaker's link	0	1	2	3
Linked audience to topic	0	1	2	3
Previewed main points/central idea	0	1	2	3

Body:

Provided adequate support materials	0	1	2	3
Orally cited appropriate sources (minimum 3)	0	1	2	3
Organized effectively	0	1	2	3
Provided smooth transitions	0	1	2	3

Conclusion:

Had "brakelight" (signaled the end)	0	1	2	3
Reviewed main points/reword central idea	0	1	2	3
Ended with strong clincher	0	1	2	3

Visual Aids:

Relevant to speech	0	1	2	3
Easy to see/read	0	1	2	3
Presented effectively	0	1	2	3
Followed professional guidelines	0	1	2	3

Speaker's Name

Class Time

Informative Speech Critique

0 Not Provided	1 Below Expectations	2 Meets Expectations	3 Exceeds Expectations

Speech Content

Introduction:

Grabbed audience's attention	0	1	2	3
Established credibility/speaker's link	0	1	2	3
Linked audience to topic	0	1	2	3
Previewed main points/central idea	0	1	2	3

Body:

Provided adequate support materials	0	1	2	3
Orally cited appropriate sources (minimum 3)	0	1	2	3
Organized effectively	0	1	2	3
Provided smooth transitions	0	1	2	3

Conclusion:

Had "brakelight" (signaled the end)	0	1	2	3
Reviewed main points/reword central idea	0	1	2	3
Ended with strong clincher	0	1	2	3

Visual Aids:

Relevant to speech	0	1	2	3
Easy to see/read	0	1	2	3
Presented effectively	0	1	2	3
Followed professional guidelines	0	1	2	3

Speaker

Eye Contact:
- Looked at all parts of audience — 0 1 2 3
- Referred to note cards appropriately — 0 1 2 3

Gestures and Posture:
- Avoided distracting mannerisms — 0 1 2 3
- Used effective gestures — 0 1 2 3
- Used appropriate facial expressions — 0 1 2 3

Voice:
- Spoke at ideal rate — 0 1 2 3
- Avoided awkward pauses — 0 1 2 3
- Sounded energetic/sincere — 0 1 2 3
- Spoke in a conversational tone — 0 1 2 3

Wording:
- Pronounced words correctly — 0 1 2 3
- Used correct grammar — 0 1 2 3
- Used appropriate word choice — 0 1 2 3
- Avoided verbal fillers (uh, um, er, okay, right, all, like, you know) — 0 1 2 3

Over-All Impressions:
- Adhered to time requirements/restrictions — 0 1 2 3
- Appeared prepared and practiced — 0 1 2 3
- Dressed appropriately — 0 1 2 3
- Used extemporaneous delivery style — 0 1 2 3

Comments:

Best aspects of speech (name at least two):

Areas for improvement:

Speaker

Eye Contact:
- Looked at all parts of audience — 0 1 2 3
- Referred to note cards appropriately — 0 1 2 3

Gestures and Posture:
- Avoided distracting mannerisms — 0 1 2 3
- Used effective gestures — 0 1 2 3
- Used appropriate facial expressions — 0 1 2 3

Voice:
- Spoke at ideal rate — 0 1 2 3
- Avoided awkward pauses — 0 1 2 3
- Sounded energetic/sincere — 0 1 2 3
- Spoke in a conversational tone — 0 1 2 3

Wording:
- Pronounced words correctly — 0 1 2 3
- Used correct grammar — 0 1 2 3
- Used appropriate word choice — 0 1 2 3
- Avoided verbal fillers (uh, um, er, okay, right, all, like, you know) — 0 1 2 3

Over-All Impressions:
- Adhered to time requirements/restrictions — 0 1 2 3
- Appeared prepared and practiced — 0 1 2 3
- Dressed appropriately — 0 1 2 3
- Used extemporaneous delivery style — 0 1 2 3

Comments:

Best aspects of speech (name at least two):

Areas for improvement:

Informative Speech Critique

0 Not Provided	1 Below Expectations	2 Meets Expectations	3 Exceeds Expectations

Speech Content

Introduction:
- Grabbed audience's attention — 0 1 2 3
- Established credibility/speaker's link — 0 1 2 3
- Linked audience to topic — 0 1 2 3
- Previewed main points/central idea — 0 1 2 3

Body:
- Provided adequate support materials — 0 1 2 3
- Orally cited appropriate sources (minimum 3) — 0 1 2 3
- Organized effectively — 0 1 2 3
- Provided smooth transitions — 0 1 2 3

Conclusion:
- Had "brakelight" (signaled the end) — 0 1 2 3
- Reviewed main points/reword central idea — 0 1 2 3
- Ended with strong clincher — 0 1 2 3

Visual Aids:
- Relevant to speech — 0 1 2 3
- Easy to see/read — 0 1 2 3
- Presented effectively — 0 1 2 3
- Followed professional guidelines — 0 1 2 3

Speaker's Name

Class Time

Informative Speech Critique

0 Not Provided	1 Below Expectations	2 Meets Expectations	3 Exceeds Expectations

Speech Content

Introduction:
- Grabbed audience's attention — 0 1 2 3
- Established credibility/speaker's link — 0 1 2 3
- Linked audience to topic — 0 1 2 3
- Previewed main points/central idea — 0 1 2 3

Body:
- Provided adequate support materials — 0 1 2 3
- Orally cited appropriate sources (minimum 3) — 0 1 2 3
- Organized effectively — 0 1 2 3
- Provided smooth transitions — 0 1 2 3

Conclusion:
- Had "brakelight" (signaled the end) — 0 1 2 3
- Reviewed main points/reword central idea — 0 1 2 3
- Ended with strong clincher — 0 1 2 3

Visual Aids:
- Relevant to speech — 0 1 2 3
- Easy to see/read — 0 1 2 3
- Presented effectively — 0 1 2 3
- Followed professional guidelines — 0 1 2 3

Speaker

Eye Contact:
- Looked at all parts of audience   0   1   2   3
- Referred to note cards appropriately   0   1   2   3

Gestures and Posture:
- Avoided distracting mannerisms   0   1   2   3
- Used effective gestures   0   1   2   3
- Used appropriate facial expressions   0   1   2   3

Voice:
- Spoke at ideal rate   0   1   2   3
- Avoided awkward pauses   0   1   2   3
- Sounded energetic/sincere   0   1   2   3
- Spoke in a conversational tone   0   1   2   3

Wording:
- Pronounced words correctly   0   1   2   3
- Used correct grammar   0   1   2   3
- Used appropriate word choice   0   1   2   3
- Avoided verbal fillers (uh, um, er, okay, right, all, like, you know)   0   1   2   3

Over-All Impressions:

- Adhered to time requirements/restrictions   0   1   2   3
- Appeared prepared and practiced   0   1   2   3
- Dressed appropriately   0   1   2   3
- Used extemporaneous delivery style   0   1   2   3

Comments:

Best aspects of speech (name at least two):

Areas for improvement:

Speaker

Eye Contact:
- Looked at all parts of audience   0   1   2   3
- Referred to note cards appropriately   0   1   2   3

Gestures and Posture:
- Avoided distracting mannerisms   0   1   2   3
- Used effective gestures   0   1   2   3
- Used appropriate facial expressions   0   1   2   3

Voice:
- Spoke at ideal rate   0   1   2   3
- Avoided awkward pauses   0   1   2   3
- Sounded energetic/sincere   0   1   2   3
- Spoke in a conversational tone   0   1   2   3

Wording:
- Pronounced words correctly   0   1   2   3
- Used correct grammar   0   1   2   3
- Used appropriate word choice   0   1   2   3
- Avoided verbal fillers (uh, um, er, okay, right, all, like, you know)   0   1   2   3

Over-All Impressions:

- Adhered to time requirements/restrictions   0   1   2   3
- Appeared prepared and practiced   0   1   2   3
- Dressed appropriately   0   1   2   3
- Used extemporaneous delivery style   0   1   2   3

Comments:

Best aspects of speech (name at least two):

Areas for improvement:

Speaker's Name _____

Class Time _____

Informative Speech Critique

0 Not Provided	1 Below Expectations	2 Meets Expectations	3 Exceeds Expectations

Speech Content

Introduction:

	0	1	2	3
• Grabbed audience's attention	0	1	2	3
• Established credibility/speaker's link	0	1	2	3
• Linked audience to topic	0	1	2	3
• Previewed main points/central idea	0	1	2	3

Body:

	0	1	2	3
• Provided adequate support materials	0	1	2	3
• Orally cited appropriate sources (minimum 3)	0	1	2	3
• Organized effectively	0	1	2	3
• Provided smooth transitions	0	1	2	3

Conclusion:

	0	1	2	3
• Had "brakelight" (signaled the end)	0	1	2	3
• Reviewed main points/reword central idea	0	1	2	3
• Ended with strong clincher	0	1	2	3

Visual Aids:

	0	1	2	3
• Relevant to speech	0	1	2	3
• Easy to see/read	0	1	2	3
• Presented effectively	0	1	2	3
• Followed professional guidelines	0	1	2	3

Speaker's Name _____

Class Time _____

Informative Speech Critique

0 Not Provided	1 Below Expectations	2 Meets Expectations	3 Exceeds Expectations

Speech Content

Introduction:

	0	1	2	3
• Grabbed audience's attention	0	1	2	3
• Established credibility/speaker's link	0	1	2	3
• Linked audience to topic	0	1	2	3
• Previewed main points/central idea	0	1	2	3

Body:

	0	1	2	3
• Provided adequate support materials	0	1	2	3
• Orally cited appropriate sources (minimum 3)	0	1	2	3
• Organized effectively	0	1	2	3
• Provided smooth transitions	0	1	2	3

Conclusion:

	0	1	2	3
• Had "brakelight" (signaled the end)	0	1	2	3
• Reviewed main points/reword central idea	0	1	2	3
• Ended with strong clincher	0	1	2	3

Visual Aids:

	0	1	2	3
• Relevant to speech	0	1	2	3
• Easy to see/read	0	1	2	3
• Presented effectively	0	1	2	3
• Followed professional guidelines	0	1	2	3

Speaker

Eye Contact:

	0	1	2	3
Looked at all parts of audience	0	1	2	3
Referred to note cards appropriately	0	1	2	3

Gestures and Posture:

	0	1	2	3
Avoided distracting mannerisms	0	1	2	3
Used effective gestures	0	1	2	3
Used appropriate facial expressions	0	1	2	3

Voice:

	0	1	2	3
Spoke at ideal rate	0	1	2	3
Avoided awkward pauses	0	1	2	3
Sounded energetic/sincere	0	1	2	3
Spoke in a conversational tone	0	1	2	3

Wording:

	0	1	2	3
Pronounced words correctly	0	1	2	3
Used correct grammar	0	1	2	3
Used appropriate word choice	0	1	2	3
Avoided verbal fillers (uh, um, er, okay, right, all, like, you know)	0	1	2	3

Over-All Impressions:

	0	1	2	3
Adhered to time requirements/restrictions	0	1	2	3
Appeared prepared and practiced	0	1	2	3
Dressed appropriately	0	1	2	3
Used extemporaneous delivery style	0	1	2	3

Comments:

Best aspects of speech (name at least two):

Areas for improvement:

Speaker

Eye Contact:

	0	1	2	3
Looked at all parts of audience	0	1	2	3
Referred to note cards appropriately	0	1	2	3

Gestures and Posture:

	0	1	2	3
Avoided distracting mannerisms	0	1	2	3
Used effective gestures	0	1	2	3
Used appropriate facial expressions	0	1	2	3

Voice:

	0	1	2	3
Spoke at ideal rate	0	1	2	3
Avoided awkward pauses	0	1	2	3
Sounded energetic/sincere	0	1	2	3
Spoke in a conversational tone	0	1	2	3

Wording:

	0	1	2	3
Pronounced words correctly	0	1	2	3
Used correct grammar	0	1	2	3
Used appropriate word choice	0	1	2	3
Avoided verbal fillers (uh, um, er, okay, right, all, like, you know)	0	1	2	3

Over-All Impressions:

	0	1	2	3
Adhered to time requirements/restrictions	0	1	2	3
Appeared prepared and practiced	0	1	2	3
Dressed appropriately	0	1	2	3
Used extemporaneous delivery style	0	1	2	3

Comments:

Best aspects of speech (name at least two):

Areas for improvement:

Speaker's Name _____

Class Time _____

Informative Speech Critique

	0 Not Provided	1 Below Expectations	2 Meets Expectations	3 Exceeds Expectations

Speech Content

Introduction:
- Grabbed audience's attention — 0 1 2 3
- Established credibility/speaker's link — 0 1 2 3
- Linked audience to topic — 0 1 2 3
- Previewed main points/central idea — 0 1 2 3

Body:
- Provided adequate support materials — 0 1 2 3
- Orally cited appropriate sources (minimum 3) — 0 1 2 3
- Organized effectively — 0 1 2 3
- Provided smooth transitions — 0 1 2 3

Conclusion:
- Had "brakelight" (signaled the end) — 0 1 2 3
- Reviewed main points/reword central idea — 0 1 2 3
- Ended with strong clincher — 0 1 2 3

Visual Aids:
- Relevant to speech — 0 1 2 3
- Easy to see/read — 0 1 2 3
- Presented effectively — 0 1 2 3
- Followed professional guidelines — 0 1 2 3

Speaker's Name _____

Class Time _____

Informative Speech Critique

	0 Not Provided	1 Below Expectations	2 Meets Expectations	3 Exceeds Expectations

Speech Content

Introduction:
- Grabbed audience's attention — 0 1 2 3
- Established credibility/speaker's link — 0 1 2 3
- Linked audience to topic — 0 1 2 3
- Previewed main points/central idea — 0 1 2 3

Body:
- Provided adequate support materials — 0 1 2 3
- Orally cited appropriate sources (minimum 3) — 0 1 2 3
- Organized effectively — 0 1 2 3
- Provided smooth transitions — 0 1 2 3

Conclusion:
- Had "brakelight" (signaled the end) — 0 1 2 3
- Reviewed main points/reword central idea — 0 1 2 3
- Ended with strong clincher — 0 1 2 3

Visual Aids:
- Relevant to speech — 0 1 2 3
- Easy to see/read — 0 1 2 3
- Presented effectively — 0 1 2 3
- Followed professional guidelines — 0 1 2 3

Speaker

Eye Contact:

- Looked at all parts of audience   0   1   2   3
- Referred to note cards appropriately   0   1   2   3

Gestures and Posture:

- Avoided distracting mannerisms   0   1   2   3
- Used effective gestures   0   1   2   3
- Used appropriate facial expressions   0   1   2   3

Voice:

- Spoke at ideal rate   0   1   2   3
- Avoided awkward pauses   0   1   2   3
- Sounded energetic/sincere   0   1   2   3
- Spoke in a conversational tone   0   1   2   3

Wording:

- Pronounced words correctly   0   1   2   3
- Used correct grammar   0   1   2   3
- Used appropriate word choice   0   1   2   3
- Avoided verbal fillers (uh, um, er, okay, right, all, like, you know)   0   1   2   3

Over-All Impressions:

- Adhered to time requirements/restrictions   0   1   2   3
- Appeared prepared and practiced   0   1   2   3
- Dressed appropriately   0   1   2   3
- Used extemporaneous delivery style   0   1   2   3

Comments:

Best aspects of speech (name at least two):

Areas for improvement:

Speaker

Eye Contact:

- Looked at all parts of audience   0   1   2   3
- Referred to note cards appropriately   0   1   2   3

Gestures and Posture:

- Avoided distracting mannerisms   0   1   2   3
- Used effective gestures   0   1   2   3
- Used appropriate facial expressions   0   1   2   3

Voice:

- Spoke at ideal rate   0   1   2   3
- Avoided awkward pauses   0   1   2   3
- Sounded energetic/sincere   0   1   2   3
- Spoke in a conversational tone   0   1   2   3

Wording:

- Pronounced words correctly   0   1   2   3
- Used correct grammar   0   1   2   3
- Used appropriate word choice   0   1   2   3
- Avoided verbal fillers (uh, um, er, okay, right, all, like, you know)   0   1   2   3

Over-All Impressions:

- Adhered to time requirements/restrictions   0   1   2   3
- Appeared prepared and practiced   0   1   2   3
- Dressed appropriately   0   1   2   3
- Used extemporaneous delivery style   0   1   2   3

Comments:

Best aspects of speech (name at least two):

Areas for improvement:

Speaker's Name _____

Class Time _____

Informative Speech Critique

0 Not Provided	1 Below Expectations	2 Meets Expectations	3 Exceeds Expectations

Speech Content

Introduction:

- Grabbed audience's attention   0 1 2 3
- Established credibility/speaker's link   0 1 2 3
- Linked audience to topic   0 1 2 3
- Previewed main points/central idea   0 1 2 3

Body:

- Provided adequate support materials   0 1 2 3
- Orally cited appropriate sources (minimum 3)   0 1 2 3
- Organized effectively   0 1 2 3
- Provided smooth transitions   0 1 2 3

Conclusion:

- Had "brakelight" (signaled the end)   0 1 2 3
- Reviewed main points/reword central idea   0 1 2 3
- Ended with strong clincher   0 1 2 3

Visual Aids:

- Relevant to speech   0 1 2 3
- Easy to see/read   0 1 2 3
- Presented effectively   0 1 2 3
- Followed professional guidelines   0 1 2 3

Speaker's Name _____

Class Time _____

Informative Speech Critique

0 Not Provided	1 Below Expectations	2 Meets Expectations	3 Exceeds Expectations

Speech Content

Introduction:

- Grabbed audience's attention   0 1 2 3
- Established credibility/speaker's link   0 1 2 3
- Linked audience to topic   0 1 2 3
- Previewed main points/central idea   0 1 2 3

Body:

- Provided adequate support materials   0 1 2 3
- Orally cited appropriate sources (minimum 3)   0 1 2 3
- Organized effectively   0 1 2 3
- Provided smooth transitions   0 1 2 3

Conclusion:

- Had "brakelight" (signaled the end)   0 1 2 3
- Reviewed main points/reword central idea   0 1 2 3
- Ended with strong clincher   0 1 2 3

Visual Aids:

- Relevant to speech   0 1 2 3
- Easy to see/read   0 1 2 3
- Presented effectively   0 1 2 3
- Followed professional guidelines   0 1 2 3

Speaker

Eye Contact:
- Looked at all parts of audience — 0 1 2 3
- Referred to note cards appropriately — 0 1 2 3

Gestures and Posture:
- Avoided distracting mannerisms — 0 1 2 3
- Used effective gestures — 0 1 2 3
- Used appropriate facial expressions — 0 1 2 3

Voice:
- Spoke at ideal rate — 0 1 2 3
- Avoided awkward pauses — 0 1 2 3
- Sounded energetic/sincere — 0 1 2 3
- Spoke in a conversational tone — 0 1 2 3

Wording:
- Pronounced words correctly — 0 1 2 3
- Used correct grammar — 0 1 2 3
- Used appropriate word choice — 0 1 2 3
- Avoided verbal fillers (uh, um, er, okay, right, all, like, you know) — 0 1 2 3

Over-All Impressions:
- Adhered to time requirements/restrictions — 0 1 2 3
- Appeared prepared and practiced — 0 1 2 3
- Dressed appropriately — 0 1 2 3
- Used extemporaneous delivery style — 0 1 2 3

Comments:

Best aspects of speech (name at least two):

Areas for improvement:

Speaker

Eye Contact:
- Looked at all parts of audience — 0 1 2 3
- Referred to note cards appropriately — 0 1 2 3

Gestures and Posture:
- Avoided distracting mannerisms — 0 1 2 3
- Used effective gestures — 0 1 2 3
- Used appropriate facial expressions — 0 1 2 3

Voice:
- Spoke at ideal rate — 0 1 2 3
- Avoided awkward pauses — 0 1 2 3
- Sounded energetic/sincere — 0 1 2 3
- Spoke in a conversational tone — 0 1 2 3

Wording:
- Pronounced words correctly — 0 1 2 3
- Used correct grammar — 0 1 2 3
- Used appropriate word choice — 0 1 2 3
- Avoided verbal fillers (uh, um, er, okay, right, all, like, you know) — 0 1 2 3

Over-All Impressions:
- Adhered to time requirements/restrictions — 0 1 2 3
- Appeared prepared and practiced — 0 1 2 3
- Dressed appropriately — 0 1 2 3
- Used extemporaneous delivery style — 0 1 2 3

Comments:

Best aspects of speech (name at least two):

Areas for improvement:

Speaker's Name _____

Class Time _____

Informative Speech Critique

0 Not Provided	1 Below Expectations	2 Meets Expectations	3 Exceeds Expectations

Speech Content

Introduction:

Item	0	1	2	3
• Grabbed audience's attention	0	1	2	3
• Established credibility/speaker's link	0	1	2	3
• Linked audience to topic	0	1	2	3
• Previewed main points/central idea	0	1	2	3

Body:

Item	0	1	2	3
• Provided adequate support materials	0	1	2	3
• Orally cited appropriate sources (minimum 3)	0	1	2	3
• Organized effectively	0	1	2	3
• Provided smooth transitions	0	1	2	3

Conclusion:

Item	0	1	2	3
• Had "brakelight" (signaled the end)	0	1	2	3
• Reviewed main points/reword central idea	0	1	2	3
• Ended with strong clincher	0	1	2	3

Visual Aids:

Item	0	1	2	3
• Relevant to speech	0	1	2	3
• Easy to see/read	0	1	2	3
• Presented effectively	0	1	2	3
• Followed professional guidelines	0	1	2	3

Speaker's Name _____

Class Time _____

Informative Speech Critique

0 Not Provided	1 Below Expectations	2 Meets Expectations	3 Exceeds Expectations

Speech Content

Introduction:

Item	0	1	2	3
• Grabbed audience's attention	0	1	2	3
• Established credibility/speaker's link	0	1	2	3
• Linked audience to topic	0	1	2	3
• Previewed main points/central idea	0	1	2	3

Body:

Item	0	1	2	3
• Provided adequate support materials	0	1	2	3
• Orally cited appropriate sources (minimum 3)	0	1	2	3
• Organized effectively	0	1	2	3
• Provided smooth transitions	0	1	2	3

Conclusion:

Item	0	1	2	3
• Had "brakelight" (signaled the end)	0	1	2	3
• Reviewed main points/reword central idea	0	1	2	3
• Ended with strong clincher	0	1	2	3

Visual Aids:

Item	0	1	2	3
• Relevant to speech	0	1	2	3
• Easy to see/read	0	1	2	3
• Presented effectively	0	1	2	3
• Followed professional guidelines	0	1	2	3

Speaker

Eye Contact:
- Looked at all parts of audience · 0 1 2 3
- Referred to note cards appropriately 0 1 2 3

Gestures and Posture:
- Avoided distracting mannerisms 0 1 2 3
- Used effective gestures 0 1 2 3
- Used appropriate facial expressions 0 1 2 3

Voice:
- Spoke at ideal rate 0 1 2 3
- Avoided awkward pauses 0 1 2 3
- Sounded energetic/sincere 0 1 2 3
- Spoke in a conversational tone 0 1 2 3

Wording:
- Pronounced words correctly 0 1 2 3
- Used correct grammar 0 1 2 3
- Used appropriate word choice 0 1 2 3
- Avoided verbal fillers (uh, um, er, okay, right, all, like, you know) 0 1 2 3

Over-All Impressions:
- Adhered to time requirements/restrictions 0 1 2 3
- Appeared prepared and practiced 0 1 2 3
- Dressed appropriately 0 1 2 3
- Used extemporaneous delivery style 0 1 2 3

Comments:

Best aspects of speech (name at least two):

Areas for improvement:

Speaker

Eye Contact:
- Looked at all parts of audience · 0 1 2 3
- Referred to note cards appropriately 0 1 2 3

Gestures and Posture:
- Avoided distracting mannerisms 0 1 2 3
- Used effective gestures 0 1 2 3
- Used appropriate facial expressions 0 1 2 3

Voice:
- Spoke at ideal rate 0 1 2 3
- Avoided awkward pauses 0 1 2 3
- Sounded energetic/sincere 0 1 2 3
- Spoke in a conversational tone 0 1 2 3

Wording:
- Pronounced words correctly 0 1 2 3
- Used correct grammar 0 1 2 3
- Used appropriate word choice 0 1 2 3
- Avoided verbal fillers (uh, um, er, okay, right, all, like, you know) 0 1 2 3

Over-All Impressions:
- Adhered to time requirements/restrictions 0 1 2 3
- Appeared prepared and practiced 0 1 2 3
- Dressed appropriately 0 1 2 3
- Used extemporaneous delivery style 0 1 2 3

Comments:

Best aspects of speech (name at least two):

Areas for improvement:

Speaker's Name _____

Class Time _____

Informative Speech Critique

	0 Not Provided	1 Below Expectations	2 Meets Expectations	3 Exceeds Expectations

Speech Content

Introduction:

- Grabbed audience's attention — 0 1 2 3
- Established credibility/speaker's link — 0 1 2 3
- Linked audience to topic — 0 1 2 3
- Previewed main points/central idea — 0 1 2 3

Body:

- Provided adequate support materials — 0 1 2 3
- Orally cited appropriate sources (minimum 3) — 0 1 2 3
- Organized effectively — 0 1 2 3
- Provided smooth transitions — 0 1 2 3

Conclusion:

- Had "brakelight" (signaled the end) — 0 1 2 3
- Reviewed main points/reword central idea — 0 1 2 3
- Ended with strong clincher — 0 1 2 3

Visual Aids:

- Relevant to speech — 0 1 2 3
- Easy to see/read — 0 1 2 3
- Presented effectively — 0 1 2 3
- Followed professional guidelines — 0 1 2 3

Speaker's Name _____

Class Time _____

Informative Speech Critique

	0 Not Provided	1 Below Expectations	2 Meets Expectations	3 Exceeds Expectations

Speech Content

Introduction:

- Grabbed audience's attention — 0 1 2 3
- Established credibility/speaker's link — 0 1 2 3
- Linked audience to topic — 0 1 2 3
- Previewed main points/central idea — 0 1 2 3

Body:

- Provided adequate support materials — 0 1 2 3
- Orally cited appropriate sources (minimum 3) — 0 1 2 3
- Organized effectively — 0 1 2 3
- Provided smooth transitions — 0 1 2 3

Conclusion:

- Had "brakelight" (signaled the end) — 0 1 2 3
- Reviewed main points/reword central idea — 0 1 2 3
- Ended with strong clincher — 0 1 2 3

Visual Aids:

- Relevant to speech — 0 1 2 3
- Easy to see/read — 0 1 2 3
- Presented effectively — 0 1 2 3
- Followed professional guidelines — 0 1 2 3

Speaker

Eye Contact:
- Looked at all parts of audience — 0 1 2 3
- Referred to note cards appropriately — 0 1 2 3

Gestures and Posture:
- Avoided distracting mannerisms — 0 1 2 3
- Used effective gestures — 0 1 2 3
- Used appropriate facial expressions — 0 1 2 3

Voice:
- Spoke at ideal rate — 0 1 2 3
- Avoided awkward pauses — 0 1 2 3
- Sounded energetic/sincere — 0 1 2 3
- Spoke in a conversational tone — 0 1 2 3

Wording:
- Pronounced words correctly — 0 1 2 3
- Used correct grammar — 0 1 2 3
- Used appropriate word choice — 0 1 2 3
- Avoided verbal fillers (uh, um, er, okay, right, all, like, you know) — 0 1 2 3

Over-All Impressions:
- Adhered to time requirements/restrictions — 0 1 2 3
- Appeared prepared and practiced — 0 1 2 3
- Dressed appropriately — 0 1 2 3
- Used extemporaneous delivery style — 0 1 2 3

Comments:

Best aspects of speech (name at least two):

Areas for improvement:

Speaker

Eye Contact:
- Looked at all parts of audience — 0 1 2 3
- Referred to note cards appropriately — 0 1 2 3

Gestures and Posture:
- Avoided distracting mannerisms — 0 1 2 3
- Used effective gestures — 0 1 2 3
- Used appropriate facial expressions — 0 1 2 3

Voice:
- Spoke at ideal rate — 0 1 2 3
- Avoided awkward pauses — 0 1 2 3
- Sounded energetic/sincere — 0 1 2 3
- Spoke in a conversational tone — 0 1 2 3

Wording:
- Pronounced words correctly — 0 1 2 3
- Used correct grammar — 0 1 2 3
- Used appropriate word choice — 0 1 2 3
- Avoided verbal fillers (uh, um, er, okay, right, all, like, you know) — 0 1 2 3

Over-All Impressions:
- Adhered to time requirements/restrictions — 0 1 2 3
- Appeared prepared and practiced — 0 1 2 3
- Dressed appropriately — 0 1 2 3
- Used extemporaneous delivery style — 0 1 2 3

Comments:

Best aspects of speech (name at least two):

Areas for improvement:

Speaker's Name _____

Class Time _____

Persuasive Speech Critique

	0 Not Provided	1 Below Expectations	2 Meets Expectations	3 Exceeds Expectations

Speech Content

Introduction:

• Grabbed audience's attention	0	1	2	3
• Established credibility/speaker's link	0	1	2	3
• Linked audience to topic	0	1	2	3
• Revealed position on issue	0	1	2	3
• Previewed main points/central idea	0	1	2	3

Body:

• Provided adequate support materials/evidence	0	1	2	3
• Orally cited appropriate sources (minimum 3)	0	1	2	3
• Organized effectively	0	1	2	3
• Provided smooth transitions	0	1	2	3

Conclusion:

• Had "brakelight" (signaled the end)	0	1	2	3
• Reviewed main points	0	1	2	3
• Ended with strong clincher	0	1	2	3
• Issued specific appeal or challenge	0	1	2	3

Visual Aids:

• Relevant to speech	0	1	2	3
• Easy to see/read	0	1	2	3
• Presented effectively	0	1	2	3
• Followed professional guidelines	0	1	2	3

Speaker's Name _____

Class Time _____

Persuasive Speech Critique

	0 Not Provided	1 Below Expectations	2 Meets Expectations	3 Exceeds Expectations

Speech Content

Introduction:

• Grabbed audience's attention	0	1	2	3
• Established credibility/speaker's link	0	1	2	3
• Linked audience to topic	0	1	2	3
• Revealed position on issue	0	1	2	3
• Previewed main points/central idea	0	1	2	3

Body:

• Provided adequate support materials/evidence	0	1	2	3
• Orally cited appropriate sources (minimum 3)	0	1	2	3
• Organized effectively	0	1	2	3
• Provided smooth transitions	0	1	2	3

Conclusion:

• Had "brakelight" (signaled the end)	0	1	2	3
• Reviewed main points	0	1	2	3
• Ended with strong clincher	0	1	2	3
• Issued specific appeal or challenge	0	1	2	3

Visual Aids:

• Relevant to speech	0	1	2	3
• Easy to see/read	0	1	2	3
• Presented effectively	0	1	2	3
• Followed professional guidelines	0	1	2	3

Speaker

Eye Contact:
- Looked at all parts of audience   0 1 2 3
- Referred to note cards appropriately   0 1 2 3

Gestures and Posture:
- Avoided distracting mannerisms   0 1 2 3
- Used effective/natural gestures   0 1 2 3
- Used appropriate facial expressions   0 1 2 3

Voice:
- Spoke at ideal rate   0 1 2 3
- Avoided awkward pauses   0 1 2 3
- Sounded energetic/sincere   0 1 2 3
- Spoke in a conversational tone   0 1 2 3

Wording:
- Pronounced words correctly   0 1 2 3
- Used correct grammar   0 1 2 3
- Used appropriate word choice   0 1 2 3
- Avoided verbal fillers (uh, um, er, okay, right, like, you know)   0 1 2 3

Over-All Impressions:
- Adhered to time requirements/restrictions   0 1 2 3
- Appeared prepared and practiced   0 1 2 3
- Dressed appropriately   0 1 2 3
- Used extemporaneous delivery   0 1 2 3

Comments:

Best aspects of speech (name at least two):

Areas for improvement:

Speaker

Eye Contact:
- Looked at all parts of audience   0 1 2 3
- Referred to note cards appropriately   0 1 2 3

Gestures and Posture:
- Avoided distracting mannerisms   0 1 2 3
- Used effective/natural gestures   0 1 2 3
- Used appropriate facial expressions   0 1 2 3

Voice:
- Spoke at ideal rate   0 1 2 3
- Avoided awkward pauses   0 1 2 3
- Sounded energetic/sincere   0 1 2 3
- Spoke in a conversational tone   0 1 2 3

Wording:
- Pronounced words correctly   0 1 2 3
- Used correct grammar   0 1 2 3
- Used appropriate word choice   0 1 2 3
- Avoided verbal fillers (uh, um, er, okay, right, like, you know)   0 1 2 3

Over-All Impressions:
- Adhered to time requirements/restrictions   0 1 2 3
- Appeared prepared and practiced   0 1 2 3
- Dressed appropriately   0 1 2 3
- Used extemporaneous delivery   0 1 2 3

Comments:

Best aspects of speech (name at least two):

Areas for improvement:

Speaker's Name _____

Class Time _____

Persuasive Speech Critique

0	1	2	3
Not Provided	Below Expectations	Meets Expectations	Exceeds Expectations

Speech Content

Introduction:

• Grabbed audience's attention	0	1	2 3
• Established credibility/speaker's link	0	1	2 3
• Linked audience to topic	0	1	2 3
• Revealed position on issue	0	1	2 3
• Previewed main points/central idea	0	1	2 3

Body:

• Provided adequate support materials/evidence	0	1	2 3
• Orally cited appropriate sources (minimum 3)	0	1	2 3
• Organized effectively	0	1	2 3
• Provided smooth transitions	0	1	2 3

Conclusion:

• Had "brakelight" (signaled the end)	0	1	2 3
• Reviewed main points	0	1	2 3
• Ended with strong clincher	0	1	2 3
• Issued specific appeal or challenge	0	1	2 3

Visual Aids:

• Relevant to speech	0	1	2 3
• Easy to see/read	0	1	2 3
• Presented effectively	0	1	2 3
• Followed professional guidelines	0	1	2 3

Speaker's Name _____

Class Time _____

Persuasive Speech Critique

0	1	2	3
Not Provided	Below Expectations	Meets Expectations	Exceeds Expectations

Speech Content

Introduction:

• Grabbed audience's attention	0	1	2 3
• Established credibility/speaker's link	0	1	2 3
• Linked audience to topic	0	1	2 3
• Revealed position on issue	0	1	2 3
• Previewed main points/central idea	0	1	2 3

Body:

• Provided adequate support materials/evidence	0	1	2 3
• Orally cited appropriate sources (minimum 3)	0	1	2 3
• Organized effectively	0	1	2 3
• Provided smooth transitions	0	1	2 3

Conclusion:

• Had "brakelight" (signaled the end)	0	1	2 3
• Reviewed main points	0	1	2 3
• Ended with strong clincher	0	1	2 3
• Issued specific appeal or challenge	0	1	2 3

Visual Aids:

• Relevant to speech	0	1	2 3
• Easy to see/read	0	1	2 3
• Presented effectively	0	1	2 3
• Followed professional guidelines	0	1	2 3

Speaker

Eye Contact:
- Looked at all parts of audience   0 1 2 3
- Referred to note cards appropriately 0 1 2 3

Gestures and Posture:
- Avoided distracting mannerisms   0 1 2 3
- Used effective/natural gestures   0 1 2 3
- Used appropriate facial expressions   0 1 2 3

Voice:
- Spoke at ideal rate   0 1 2 3
- Avoided awkward pauses   0 1 2 3
- Sounded energetic/sincere   0 1 2 3
- Spoke in a conversational tone   0 1 2 3

Wording:
- Pronounced words correctly   0 1 2 3
- Used correct grammar   0 1 2 3
- Used appropriate word choice   0 1 2 3
- Avoided verbal fillers (uh, um, er, okay, right, like, you know)   0 1 2 3

Over-All Impressions:
- Adhered to time requirements/restrictions   0 1 2 3
- Appeared prepared and practiced   0 1 2 3
- Dressed appropriately   0 1 2 3
- Used extemporaneous delivery   0 1 2 3

Comments:

Best aspects of speech (name at least two):

Areas for improvement:

Speaker

Eye Contact:
- Looked at all parts of audience   0 1 2 3
- Referred to note cards appropriately 0 1 2 3

Gestures and Posture:
- Avoided distracting mannerisms   0 1 2 3
- Used effective/natural gestures   0 1 2 3
- Used appropriate facial expressions   0 1 2 3

Voice:
- Spoke at ideal rate   0 1 2 3
- Avoided awkward pauses   0 1 2 3
- Sounded energetic/sincere   0 1 2 3
- Spoke in a conversational tone   0 1 2 3

Wording:
- Pronounced words correctly   0 1 2 3
- Used correct grammar   0 1 2 3
- Used appropriate word choice   0 1 2 3
- Avoided verbal fillers (uh, um, er, okay, right, like, you know)   0 1 2 3

Over-All Impressions:
- Adhered to time requirements/restrictions   0 1 2 3
- Appeared prepared and practiced   0 1 2 3
- Dressed appropriately   0 1 2 3
- Used extemporaneous delivery   0 1 2 3

Comments:

Best aspects of speech (name at least two):

Areas for improvement:

Persuasive Speech Critique

0 Not Provided	1 Below Expectations	2 Meets Expectations	3 Exceeds Expectations

Speech Content

Introduction:
- Grabbed audience's attention   0 1 2 3
- Established credibility/speaker's link   0 1 2 3
- Linked audience to topic   0 1 2 3
- Revealed position on issue   0 1 2 3
- Previewed main points/central idea   0 1 2 3

Body:
- Provided adequate support materials/evidence   0 1 2 3
- Orally cited appropriate sources (minimum 3)   0 1 2 3
- Organized effectively   0 1 2 3
- Provided smooth transitions   0 1 2 3

Conclusion:
- Had "brakelight" (signaled the end)   0 1 2 3
- Reviewed main points   0 1 2 3
- Ended with strong clincher   0 1 2 3
- Issued specific appeal or challenge   0 1 2 3

Visual Aids:
- Relevant to speech   0 1 2 3
- Easy to see/read   0 1 2 3
- Presented effectively   0 1 2 3
- Followed professional guidelines   0 1 2 3

Speaker's Name _____

Class Time _____

Persuasive Speech Critique

0 Not Provided	1 Below Expectations	2 Meets Expectations	3 Exceeds Expectations

Speech Content

Introduction:
- Grabbed audience's attention   0 1 2 3
- Established credibility/speaker's link   0 1 2 3
- Linked audience to topic   0 1 2 3
- Revealed position on issue   0 1 2 3
- Previewed main points/central idea   0 1 2 3

Body:
- Provided adequate support materials/evidence   0 1 2 3
- Orally cited appropriate sources (minimum 3)   0 1 2 3
- Organized effectively   0 1 2 3
- Provided smooth transitions   0 1 2 3

Conclusion:
- Had "brakelight" (signaled the end)   0 1 2 3
- Reviewed main points   0 1 2 3
- Ended with strong clincher   0 1 2 3
- Issued specific appeal or challenge   0 1 2 3

Visual Aids:
- Relevant to speech   0 1 2 3
- Easy to see/read   0 1 2 3
- Presented effectively   0 1 2 3
- Followed professional guidelines   0 1 2 3

Speaker

Eye Contact:

	0	1	2	3
Looked at all parts of audience	0	1	2	3
Referred to note cards appropriately	0	1	2	3

Gestures and Posture:

	0	1	2	3
Avoided distracting mannerisms	0	1	2	3
Used effective/natural gestures	0	1	2	3
Used appropriate facial expressions	0	1	2	3

Voice:

	0	1	2	3
Spoke at ideal rate	0	1	2	3
Avoided awkward pauses	0	1	2	3
Sounded energetic/sincere	0	1	2	3
Spoke in a conversational tone	0	1	2	3

Wording:

	0	1	2	3
Pronounced words correctly	0	1	2	3
Used correct grammar	0	1	2	3
Used appropriate word choice	0	1	2	3
Avoided verbal fillers (uh, um, er, okay, right, like, you know)	0	1	2	3

Over-All Impressions:

	0	1	2	3
Adhered to time requirements/restrictions	0	1	2	3
Appeared prepared and practiced	0	1	2	3
Dressed appropriately	0	1	2	3
Used extemporaneous delivery	0	1	2	3

Comments:

Best aspects of speech (name at least two):

Areas for improvement:

Speaker

Eye Contact:

	0	1	2	3
Looked at all parts of audience	0	1	2	3
Referred to note cards appropriately	0	1	2	3

Gestures and Posture:

	0	1	2	3
Avoided distracting mannerisms	0	1	2	3
Used effective/natural gestures	0	1	2	3
Used appropriate facial expressions	0	1	2	3

Voice:

	0	1	2	3
Spoke at ideal rate	0	1	2	3
Avoided awkward pauses	0	1	2	3
Sounded energetic/sincere	0	1	2	3
Spoke in a conversational tone	0	1	2	3

Wording:

	0	1	2	3
Pronounced words correctly	0	1	2	3
Used correct grammar	0	1	2	3
Used appropriate word choice	0	1	2	3
Avoided verbal fillers (uh, um, er, okay, right, like, you know)	0	1	2	3

Over-All Impressions:

	0	1	2	3
Adhered to time requirements/restrictions	0	1	2	3
Appeared prepared and practiced	0	1	2	3
Dressed appropriately	0	1	2	3
Used extemporaneous delivery	0	1	2	3

Comments:

Best aspects of speech (name at least two):

Areas for improvement:

Speaker's Name _____

Class Time _____

Persuasive Speech Critique

0 Not Provided	1 Below Expectations	2 Meets Expectations	3 Exceeds Expectations

Speech Content

Introduction:

• Grabbed audience's attention	0	1	2	3
• Established credibility/speaker's link	0	1	2	3
• Linked audience to topic	0	1	2	3
• Revealed position on issue	0	1	2	3
• Previewed main points/central idea	0	1	2	3

Body:

• Provided adequate support materials/evidence	0	1	2	3
• Orally cited appropriate sources (minimum 3)	0	1	2	3
• Organized effectively	0	1	2	3
• Provided smooth transitions	0	1	2	3

Conclusion:

• Had "brakelight" (signaled the end)	0	1	2	3
• Reviewed main points	0	1	2	3
• Ended with strong clincher	0	1	2	3
• Issued specific appeal or challenge	0	1	2	3

Visual Aids:

• Relevant to speech	0	1	2	3
• Easy to see/read	0	1	2	3
• Presented effectively	0	1	2	3
• Followed professional guidelines	0	1	2	3

Speaker's Name _____

Class Time _____

Persuasive Speech Critique

0 Not Provided	1 Below Expectations	2 Meets Expectations	3 Exceeds Expectations

Speech Content

Introduction:

• Grabbed audience's attention	0	1	2	3
• Established credibility/speaker's link	0	1	2	3
• Linked audience to topic	0	1	2	3
• Revealed position on issue	0	1	2	3
• Previewed main points/central idea	0	1	2	3

Body:

• Provided adequate support materials/evidence	0	1	2	3
• Orally cited appropriate sources (minimum 3)	0	1	2	3
• Organized effectively	0	1	2	3
• Provided smooth transitions	0	1	2	3

Conclusion:

• Had "brakelight" (signaled the end)	0	1	2	3
• Reviewed main points	0	1	2	3
• Ended with strong clincher	0	1	2	3
• Issued specific appeal or challenge	0	1	2	3

Visual Aids:

• Relevant to speech	0	1	2	3
• Easy to see/read	0	1	2	3
• Presented effectively	0	1	2	3
• Followed professional guidelines	0	1	2	3

Speaker

Eye Contact:
- Looked at all parts of audience 0 1 2 3
- Referred to note cards appropriately 0 1 2 3

Gestures and Posture:
- Avoided distracting mannerisms 0 1 2 3
- Used effective/natural gestures 0 1 2 3
- Used appropriate facial expressions 0 1 2 3

Voice:
- Spoke at ideal rate 0 1 2 3
- Avoided awkward pauses 0 1 2 3
- Sounded energetic/sincere 0 1 2 3
- Spoke in a conversational tone 0 1 2 3

Wording:
- Pronounced words correctly 0 1 2 3
- Used correct grammar 0 1 2 3
- Used appropriate word choice 0 1 2 3
- Avoided verbal fillers (uh, um, er, okay, right, like, you know) 0 1 2 3

Over-All Impressions:
- Adhered to time requirements/restrictions 0 1 2 3
- Appeared prepared and practiced 0 1 2 3
- Dressed appropriately 0 1 2 3
- Used extemporaneous delivery 0 1 2 3

Comments:

Best aspects of speech (name at least two):

Areas for improvement:

Speaker

Eye Contact:
- Looked at all parts of audience 0 1 2 3
- Referred to note cards appropriately 0 1 2 3

Gestures and Posture:
- Avoided distracting mannerisms 0 1 2 3
- Used effective/natural gestures 0 1 2 3
- Used appropriate facial expressions 0 1 2 3

Voice:
- Spoke at ideal rate 0 1 2 3
- Avoided awkward pauses 0 1 2 3
- Sounded energetic/sincere 0 1 2 3
- Spoke in a conversational tone 0 1 2 3

Wording:
- Pronounced words correctly 0 1 2 3
- Used correct grammar 0 1 2 3
- Used appropriate word choice 0 1 2 3
- Avoided verbal fillers (uh, um, er, okay, right, like, you know) 0 1 2 3

Over-All Impressions:
- Adhered to time requirements/restrictions 0 1 2 3
- Appeared prepared and practiced 0 1 2 3
- Dressed appropriately 0 1 2 3
- Used extemporaneous delivery 0 1 2 3

Comments:

Best aspects of speech (name at least two):

Areas for improvement:

Speaker's Name _____

Class Time _____

Persuasive Speech Critique

0	1	2	3
Not Provided	Below Expectations	Meets Expectations	Exceeds Expectations

Speech Content

Introduction:
- Grabbed audience's attention   0 1 2 3
- Established credibility/speaker's link   0 1 2 3
- Linked audience to topic   0 1 2 3
- Revealed position on issue   0 1 2 3
- Previewed main points/central idea   0 1 2 3

Body:
- Provided adequate support materials/evidence   0 1 2 3
- Orally cited appropriate sources (minimum 3)   0 1 2 3
- Organized effectively   0 1 2 3
- Provided smooth transitions   0 1 2 3

Conclusion:
- Had "brakelight" (signaled the end)   0 1 2 3
- Reviewed main points   0 1 2 3
- Ended with strong clincher   0 1 2 3
- Issued specific appeal or challenge   0 1 2 3

Visual Aids:
- Relevant to speech   0 1 2 3
- Easy to see/read   0 1 2 3
- Presented effectively   0 1 2 3
- Followed professional guidelines   0 1 2 3

Speaker's Name _____

Class Time _____

Persuasive Speech Critique

0	1	2	3
Not Provided	Below Expectations	Meets Expectations	Exceeds Expectations

Speech Content

Introduction:
- Grabbed audience's attention   0 1 2 3
- Established credibility/speaker's link   0 1 2 3
- Linked audience to topic   0 1 2 3
- Revealed position on issue   0 1 2 3
- Previewed main points/central idea   0 1 2 3

Body:
- Provided adequate support materials/evidence   0 1 2 3
- Orally cited appropriate sources (minimum 3)   0 1 2 3
- Organized effectively   0 1 2 3
- Provided smooth transitions   0 1 2 3

Conclusion:
- Had "brakelight" (signaled the end)   0 1 2 3
- Reviewed main points   0 1 2 3
- Ended with strong clincher   0 1 2 3
- Issued specific appeal or challenge   0 1 2 3

Visual Aids:
- Relevant to speech   0 1 2 3
- Easy to see/read   0 1 2 3
- Presented effectively   0 1 2 3
- Followed professional guidelines   0 1 2 3

Speaker

Eye Contact:
- Looked at all parts of audience — 0 1 2 3
- Referred to note cards appropriately — 0 1 2 3

Gestures and Posture:
- Avoided distracting mannerisms — 0 1 2 3
- Used effective/natural gestures — 0 1 2 3
- Used appropriate facial expressions — 0 1 2 3

Voice:
- Spoke at ideal rate — 0 1 2 3
- Avoided awkward pauses — 0 1 2 3
- Sounded energetic/sincere — 0 1 2 3
- Spoke in a conversational tone — 0 1 2 3

Wording:
- Pronounced words correctly — 0 1 2 3
- Used correct grammar — 0 1 2 3
- Used appropriate word choice — 0 1 2 3
- Avoided verbal fillers (uh, um, er, okay, right, like, you know) — 0 1 2 3

Over-All Impressions:
- Adhered to time requirements/restrictions — 0 1 2 3
- Appeared prepared and practiced — 0 1 2 3
- Dressed appropriately — 0 1 2 3
- Used extemporaneous delivery — 0 1 2 3

Comments:

Best aspects of speech (name at least two):

Areas for improvement:

Speaker

Eye Contact:
- Looked at all parts of audience — 0 1 2 3
- Referred to note cards appropriately — 0 1 2 3

Gestures and Posture:
- Avoided distracting mannerisms — 0 1 2 3
- Used effective/natural gestures — 0 1 2 3
- Used appropriate facial expressions — 0 1 2 3

Voice:
- Spoke at ideal rate — 0 1 2 3
- Avoided awkward pauses — 0 1 2 3
- Sounded energetic/sincere — 0 1 2 3
- Spoke in a conversational tone — 0 1 2 3

Wording:
- Pronounced words correctly — 0 1 2 3
- Used correct grammar — 0 1 2 3
- Used appropriate word choice — 0 1 2 3
- Avoided verbal fillers (uh, um, er, okay, right, like, you know) — 0 1 2 3

Over-All Impressions:
- Adhered to time requirements/restrictions — 0 1 2 3
- Appeared prepared and practiced — 0 1 2 3
- Dressed appropriately — 0 1 2 3
- Used extemporaneous delivery — 0 1 2 3

Comments:

Best aspects of speech (name at least two):

Areas for improvement:

Persuasive Speech Critique

0 Not Provided	1 Below Expectations	2 Meets Expectations	3 Exceeds Expectations

Speech Content

Introduction:

• Grabbed audience's attention	0	1	2 3
• Established credibility/speaker's link	0	1	2 3
• Linked audience to topic	0	1	2 3
• Revealed position on issue	0	1	2 3
• Previewed main points/central idea	0	1	2 3

Body:

• Provided adequate support materials/evidence	0	1	2 3
• Orally cited appropriate sources (minimum 3)	0	1	2 3
• Organized effectively	0	1	2 3
• Provided smooth transitions	0	1	2 3

Conclusion:

• Had "brakelight" (signaled the end)	0	1	2 3
• Reviewed main points	0	1	2 3
• Ended with strong clincher	0	1	2 3
• Issued specific appeal or challenge	0	1	2 3

Visual Aids:

• Relevant to speech	0	1	2 3
• Easy to see/read	0	1	2 3
• Presented effectively	0	1	2 3
• Followed professional guidelines	0	1	2 3

Speaker's Name _____

Class Time _____

Persuasive Speech Critique

0 Not Provided	1 Below Expectations	2 Meets Expectations	3 Exceeds Expectations

Speech Content

Introduction:

• Grabbed audience's attention	0	1	2 3
• Established credibility/speaker's link	0	1	2 3
• Linked audience to topic	0	1	2 3
• Revealed position on issue	0	1	2 3
• Previewed main points/central idea	0	1	2 3

Body:

• Provided adequate support materials/evidence	0	1	2 3
• Orally cited appropriate sources (minimum 3)	0	1	2 3
• Organized effectively	0	1	2 3
• Provided smooth transitions	0	1	2 3

Conclusion:

• Had "brakelight" (signaled the end)	0	1	2 3
• Reviewed main points	0	1	2 3
• Ended with strong clincher	0	1	2 3
• Issued specific appeal or challenge	0	1	2 3

Visual Aids:

• Relevant to speech	0	1	2 3
• Easy to see/read	0	1	2 3
• Presented effectively	0	1	2 3
• Followed professional guidelines	0	1	2 3

Speaker

Eye Contact:

• Looked at all parts of audience	0	1	2	3
• Referred to note cards appropriately	0	1	2	3

Gestures and Posture:

• Avoided distracting mannerisms	0	1	2	3
• Used effective/natural gestures	0	1	2	3
• Used appropriate facial expressions	0	1	2	3

Voice:

• Spoke at ideal rate	0	1	2	3
• Avoided awkward pauses	0	1	2	3
• Sounded energetic/sincere	0	1	2	3
• Spoke in a conversational tone	0	1	2	3

Wording:

• Pronounced words correctly	0	1	2	3
• Used correct grammar	0	1	2	3
• Used appropriate word choice	0	1	2	3
• Avoided verbal fillers (uh, um, er, okay, right, like, you know)	0	1	2	3

Over-All Impressions:

• Adhered to time requirements/restrictions	0	1	2	3
• Appeared prepared and practiced	0	1	2	3
• Dressed appropriately	0	1	2	3
• Used extemporaneous delivery	0	1	2	3

Comments:

Best aspects of speech (name at least two):

Areas for improvement:

Speaker

Eye Contact:

• Looked at all parts of audience	0	1	2	3
• Referred to note cards appropriately	0	1	2	3

Gestures and Posture:

• Avoided distracting mannerisms	0	1	2	3
• Used effective/natural gestures	0	1	2	3
• Used appropriate facial expressions	0	1	2	3

Voice:

• Spoke at ideal rate	0	1	2	3
• Avoided awkward pauses	0	1	2	3
• Sounded energetic/sincere	0	1	2	3
• Spoke in a conversational tone	0	1	2	3

Wording:

• Pronounced words correctly	0	1	2	3
• Used correct grammar	0	1	2	3
• Used appropriate word choice	0	1	2	3
• Avoided verbal fillers (uh, um, er, okay, right, like, you know)	0	1	2	3

Over-All Impressions:

• Adhered to time requirements/restrictions	0	1	2	3
• Appeared prepared and practiced	0	1	2	3
• Dressed appropriately	0	1	2	3
• Used extemporaneous delivery	0	1	2	3

Comments:

Best aspects of speech (name at least two):

Areas for improvement:

Speaker's Name _____

Class Time _____

Persuasive Speech Critique

0	1	2	3
Not Provided	Below Expectations	Meets Expectations	Exceeds Expectations

Speech Content

Introduction:

- Grabbed audience's attention — 0 1 2 3
- Established credibility/speaker's link — 0 1 2 3
- Linked audience to topic — 0 1 2 3
- Revealed position on issue — 0 1 2 3
- Previewed main points/central idea — 0 1 2 3

Body:

- Provided adequate support materials/evidence — 0 1 2 3
- Orally cited appropriate sources (minimum 3) — 0 1 2 3
- Organized effectively — 0 1 2 3
- Provided smooth transitions — 0 1 2 3

Conclusion:

- Had "brakelight" (signaled the end) — 0 1 2 3
- Reviewed main points — 0 1 2 3
- Ended with strong clincher — 0 1 2 3
- Issued specific appeal or challenge — 0 1 2 3

Visual Aids:

- Relevant to speech — 0 1 2 3
- Easy to see/read — 0 1 2 3
- Presented effectively — 0 1 2 3
- Followed professional guidelines — 0 1 2 3

Speaker's Name _____

Class Time _____

Persuasive Speech Critique

0	1	2	3
Not Provided	Below Expectations	Meets Expectations	Exceeds Expectations

Speech Content

Introduction:

- Grabbed audience's attention — 0 1 2 3
- Established credibility/speaker's link — 0 1 2 3
- Linked audience to topic — 0 1 2 3
- Revealed position on issue — 0 1 2 3
- Previewed main points/central idea — 0 1 2 3

Body:

- Provided adequate support materials/evidence — 0 1 2 3
- Orally cited appropriate sources (minimum 3) — 0 1 2 3
- Organized effectively — 0 1 2 3
- Provided smooth transitions — 0 1 2 3

Conclusion:

- Had "brakelight" (signaled the end) — 0 1 2 3
- Reviewed main points — 0 1 2 3
- Ended with strong clincher — 0 1 2 3
- Issued specific appeal or challenge — 0 1 2 3

Visual Aids:

- Relevant to speech — 0 1 2 3
- Easy to see/read — 0 1 2 3
- Presented effectively — 0 1 2 3
- Followed professional guidelines — 0 1 2 3

Speaker

Eye Contact:

• Looked at all parts of audience	0	1	2	3
• Referred to note cards appropriately	0	1	2	3

Gestures and Posture:

• Avoided distracting mannerisms	0	1	2	3
• Used effective/natural gestures	0	1	2	3
• Used appropriate facial expressions	0	1	2	3

Voice:

• Spoke at ideal rate	0	1	2	3
• Avoided awkward pauses	0	1	2	3
• Sounded energetic/sincere	0	1	2	3
• Spoke in a conversational tone	0	1	2	3

Wording:

• Pronounced words correctly	0	1	2	3
• Used correct grammar	0	1	2	3
• Used appropriate word choice	0	1	2	3
• Avoided verbal fillers (uh, um, er, okay, right, like, you know)	0	1	2	3

Over-All Impressions:

• Adhered to time requirements/restrictions	0	1	2	3
• Appeared prepared and practiced	0	1	2	3
• Dressed appropriately	0	1	2	3
• Used extemporaneous delivery	0	1	2	3

Comments:

Best aspects of speech (name at least two):

Areas for improvement:

Speaker

Eye Contact:

• Looked at all parts of audience	0	1	2	3
• Referred to note cards appropriately	0	1	2	3

Gestures and Posture:

• Avoided distracting mannerisms	0	1	2	3
• Used effective/natural gestures	0	1	2	3
• Used appropriate facial expressions	0	1	2	3

Voice:

• Spoke at ideal rate	0	1	2	3
• Avoided awkward pauses	0	1	2	3
• Sounded energetic/sincere	0	1	2	3
• Spoke in a conversational tone	0	1	2	3

Wording:

• Pronounced words correctly	0	1	2	3
• Used correct grammar	0	1	2	3
• Used appropriate word choice	0	1	2	3
• Avoided verbal fillers (uh, um, er, okay, right, like, you know)	0	1	2	3

Over-All Impressions:

• Adhered to time requirements/restrictions	0	1	2	3
• Appeared prepared and practiced	0	1	2	3
• Dressed appropriately	0	1	2	3
• Used extemporaneous delivery	0	1	2	3

Comments:

Best aspects of speech (name at least two):

Areas for improvement:

Speaker's Name _____

Class Time _____

Persuasive Speech Critique

	0 Not Provided	1 Below Expectations	2 Meets Expectations	3 Exceeds Expectations

Speech Content

Introduction:

Grabbed audience's attention	0	1	2	3
Established credibility/speaker's link	0	1	2	3
Linked audience to topic	0	1	2	3
Revealed position on issue	0	1	2	3
Previewed main points/central idea	0	1	2	3

Body:

Provided adequate support materials/evidence	0	1	2	3
Orally cited appropriate sources (minimum 3)	0	1	2	3
Organized effectively	0	1	2	3
Provided smooth transitions	0	1	2	3

Conclusion:

Had "brakelight" (signaled the end)	0	1	2	3
Reviewed main points	0	1	2	3
Ended with strong clincher	0	1	2	3
Issued specific appeal or challenge	0	1	2	3

Visual Aids:

Relevant to speech	0	1	2	3
Easy to see/read	0	1	2	3
Presented effectively	0	1	2	3
Followed professional guidelines	0	1	2	3

Speaker's Name _____

Class Time _____

Persuasive Speech Critique

	0 Not Provided	1 Below Expectations	2 Meets Expectations	3 Exceeds Expectations

Speech Content

Introduction:

Grabbed audience's attention	0	1	2	3
Established credibility/speaker's link	0	1	2	3
Linked audience to topic	0	1	2	3
Revealed position on issue	0	1	2	3
Previewed main points/central idea	0	1	2	3

Body:

Provided adequate support materials/evidence	0	1	2	3
Orally cited appropriate sources (minimum 3)	0	1	2	3
Organized effectively	0	1	2	3
Provided smooth transitions	0	1	2	3

Conclusion:

Had "brakelight" (signaled the end)	0	1	2	3
Reviewed main points	0	1	2	3
Ended with strong clincher	0	1	2	3
Issued specific appeal or challenge	0	1	2	3

Visual Aids:

Relevant to speech	0	1	2	3
Easy to see/read	0	1	2	3
Presented effectively	0	1	2	3
Followed professional guidelines	0	1	2	3

Speaker

Eye Contact:
- Looked at all parts of audience   0   1   2   3
- Referred to note cards appropriately   0   1   2   3

Gestures and Posture:
- Avoided distracting mannerisms   0   1   2   3
- Used effective/natural gestures   0   1   2   3
- Used appropriate facial expressions   0   1   2   3

Voice:
- Spoke at ideal rate   0   1   2   3
- Avoided awkward pauses   0   1   2   3
- Sounded energetic/sincere   0   1   2   3
- Spoke in a conversational tone   0   1   2   3

Wording:
- Pronounced words correctly   0   1   2   3
- Used correct grammar   0   1   2   3
- Used appropriate word choice   0   1   2   3
- Avoided verbal fillers (uh, um, er, okay, right, like, you know)   0   1   2   3

Over-All Impressions:
- Adhered to time requirements/restrictions   0   1   2   3
- Appeared prepared and practiced   0   1   2   3
- Dressed appropriately   0   1   2   3
- Used extemporaneous delivery   0   1   2   3

Comments:

Best aspects of speech (name at least two):

Areas for improvement:

Speaker

Eye Contact:
- Looked at all parts of audience   0   1   2   3
- Referred to note cards appropriately   0   1   2   3

Gestures and Posture:
- Avoided distracting mannerisms   0   1   2   3
- Used effective/natural gestures   0   1   2   3
- Used appropriate facial expressions   0   1   2   3

Voice:
- Spoke at ideal rate   0   1   2   3
- Avoided awkward pauses   0   1   2   3
- Sounded energetic/sincere   0   1   2   3
- Spoke in a conversational tone   0   1   2   3

Wording:
- Pronounced words correctly   0   1   2   3
- Used correct grammar   0   1   2   3
- Used appropriate word choice   0   1   2   3
- Avoided verbal fillers (uh, um, er, okay, right, like, you know)   0   1   2   3

Over-All Impressions:
- Adhered to time requirements/restrictions   0   1   2   3
- Appeared prepared and practiced   0   1   2   3
- Dressed appropriately   0   1   2   3
- Used extemporaneous delivery   0   1   2   3

Comments:

Best aspects of speech (name at least two):

Areas for improvement:

Speaker's Name _____

Class Time _____

Persuasive Speech Critique

0 Not Provided	1 Below Expectations	2 Meets Expectations	3 Exceeds Expectations

Speech Content

Introduction:

• Grabbed audience's attention	0	1	2	3
• Established credibility/speaker's link	0	1	2	3
• Linked audience to topic	0	1	2	3
• Revealed position on issue	0	1	2	3
• Previewed main points/central idea	0	1	2	3

Body:

• Provided adequate support materials/evidence	0	1	2	3
• Orally cited appropriate sources (minimum 3)	0	1	2	3
• Organized effectively	0	1	2	3
• Provided smooth transitions	0	1	2	3

Conclusion:

• Had "brakelight" (signaled the end)	0	1	2	3
• Reviewed main points	0	1	2	3
• Ended with strong clincher	0	1	2	3
• Issued specific appeal or challenge	0	1	2	3

Visual Aids:

• Relevant to speech	0	1	2	3
• Easy to see/read	0	1	2	3
• Presented effectively	0	1	2	3
• Followed professional guidelines	0	1	2	3

Speaker's Name _____

Class Time _____

Persuasive Speech Critique

0 Not Provided	1 Below Expectations	2 Meets Expectations	3 Exceeds Expectations

Speech Content

Introduction:

• Grabbed audience's attention	0	1	2	3
• Established credibility/speaker's link	0	1	2	3
• Linked audience to topic	0	1	2	3
• Revealed position on issue	0	1	2	3
• Previewed main points/central idea	0	1	2	3

Body:

• Provided adequate support materials/evidence	0	1	2	3
• Orally cited appropriate sources (minimum 3)	0	1	2	3
• Organized effectively	0	1	2	3
• Provided smooth transitions	0	1	2	3

Conclusion:

• Had "brakelight" (signaled the end)	0	1	2	3
• Reviewed main points	0	1	2	3
• Ended with strong clincher	0	1	2	3
• Issued specific appeal or challenge	0	1	2	3

Visual Aids:

• Relevant to speech	0	1	2	3
• Easy to see/read	0	1	2	3
• Presented effectively	0	1	2	3
• Followed professional guidelines	0	1	2	3

Speaker

Eye Contact:
- Looked at all parts of audience   0 1 2 3
- Referred to note cards appropriately   0 1 2 3

Gestures and Posture:
- Avoided distracting mannerisms   0 1 2 3
- Used effective/natural gestures   0 1 2 3
- Used appropriate facial expressions   0 1 2 3

Voice:
- Spoke at ideal rate   0 1 2 3
- Avoided awkward pauses   0 1 2 3
- Sounded energetic/sincere   0 1 2 3
- Spoke in a conversational tone   0 1 2 3

Wording:
- Pronounced words correctly   0 1 2 3
- Used correct grammar   0 1 2 3
- Used appropriate word choice   0 1 2 3
- Avoided verbal fillers (uh, um, er, okay, right, like, you know)   0 1 2 3

Over-All Impressions:
- Adhered to time requirements/restrictions   0 1 2 3
- Appeared prepared and practiced   0 1 2 3
- Dressed appropriately   0 1 2 3
- Used extemporaneous delivery   0 1 2 3

Comments:

Best aspects of speech (name at least two):

Areas for improvement:

Speaker

Eye Contact:
- Looked at all parts of audience   0 1 2 3
- Referred to note cards appropriately   0 1 2 3

Gestures and Posture:
- Avoided distracting mannerisms   0 1 2 3
- Used effective/natural gestures   0 1 2 3
- Used appropriate facial expressions   0 1 2 3

Voice:
- Spoke at ideal rate   0 1 2 3
- Avoided awkward pauses   0 1 2 3
- Sounded energetic/sincere   0 1 2 3
- Spoke in a conversational tone   0 1 2 3

Wording:
- Pronounced words correctly   0 1 2 3
- Used correct grammar   0 1 2 3
- Used appropriate word choice   0 1 2 3
- Avoided verbal fillers (uh, um, er, okay, right, like, you know)   0 1 2 3

Over-All Impressions:
- Adhered to time requirements/restrictions   0 1 2 3
- Appeared prepared and practiced   0 1 2 3
- Dressed appropriately   0 1 2 3
- Used extemporaneous delivery   0 1 2 3

Comments:

Best aspects of speech (name at least two):

Areas for improvement:

Speaker's Name _____

Class Time _____

Persuasive Speech Critique

0 Not Provided	1 Below Expectations	2 Meets Expectations	3 Exceeds Expectations

Speech Content

Introduction:

• Grabbed audience's attention	0	1	2	3
• Established credibility/speaker's link	0	1	2	3
• Linked audience to topic	0	1	2	3
• Revealed position on issue	0	1	2	3
• Previewed main points/central idea	0	1	2	3

Body:

• Provided adequate support materials/evidence	0	1	2	3
• Orally cited appropriate sources (minimum 3)	0	1	2	3
• Organized effectively	0	1	2	3
• Provided smooth transitions	0	1	2	3

Conclusion:

• Had "brakelight" (signaled the end)	0	1	2	3
• Reviewed main points	0	1	2	3
• Ended with strong clincher	0	1	2	3
• Issued specific appeal or challenge	0	1	2	3

Visual Aids:

• Relevant to speech	0	1	2	3
• Easy to see/read	0	1	2	3
• Presented effectively	0	1	2	3
• Followed professional guidelines	0	1	2	3

Speaker's Name _____

Class Time _____

Persuasive Speech Critique

0 Not Provided	1 Below Expectations	2 Meets Expectations	3 Exceeds Expectations

Speech Content

Introduction:

• Grabbed audience's attention	0	1	2	3
• Established credibility/speaker's link	0	1	2	3
• Linked audience to topic	0	1	2	3
• Revealed position on issue	0	1	2	3
• Previewed main points/central idea	0	1	2	3

Body:

• Provided adequate support materials/evidence	0	1	2	3
• Orally cited appropriate sources (minimum 3)	0	1	2	3
• Organized effectively	0	1	2	3
• Provided smooth transitions	0	1	2	3

Conclusion:

• Had "brakelight" (signaled the end)	0	1	2	3
• Reviewed main points	0	1	2	3
• Ended with strong clincher	0	1	2	3
• Issued specific appeal or challenge	0	1	2	3

Visual Aids:

• Relevant to speech	0	1	2	3
• Easy to see/read	0	1	2	3
• Presented effectively	0	1	2	3
• Followed professional guidelines	0	1	2	3

Speaker

Eye Contact:

- Looked at all parts of audience   0   1   2   3
- Referred to note cards appropriately   0   1   2   3

Gestures and Posture:

- Avoided distracting mannerisms   0   1   2   3
- Used effective/natural gestures   0   1   2   3
- Used appropriate facial expressions   0   1   2   3

Voice:

- Spoke at ideal rate   0   1   2   3
- Avoided awkward pauses   0   1   2   3
- Sounded energetic/sincere   0   1   2   3
- Spoke in a conversational tone   0   1   2   3

Wording:

- Pronounced words correctly   0   1   2   3
- Used correct grammar   0   1   2   3
- Used appropriate word choice   0   1   2   3
- Avoided verbal fillers (uh, um, er, okay, right, like, you know)   0   1   2   3

Over-All Impressions:

- Adhered to time requirements/restrictions   0   1   2   3
- Appeared prepared and practiced   0   1   2   3
- Dressed appropriately   0   1   2   3
- Used extemporaneous delivery   0   1   2   3

Comments:

Best aspects of speech (name at least two):

Areas for improvement:

Speaker

Eye Contact:

- Looked at all parts of audience   0   1   2   3
- Referred to note cards appropriately   0   1   2   3

Gestures and Posture:

- Avoided distracting mannerisms   0   1   2   3
- Used effective/natural gestures   0   1   2   3
- Used appropriate facial expressions   0   1   2   3

Voice:

- Spoke at ideal rate   0   1   2   3
- Avoided awkward pauses   0   1   2   3
- Sounded energetic/sincere   0   1   2   3
- Spoke in a conversational tone   0   1   2   3

Wording:

- Pronounced words correctly   0   1   2   3
- Used correct grammar   0   1   2   3
- Used appropriate word choice   0   1   2   3
- Avoided verbal fillers (uh, um, er, okay, right, like, you know)   0   1   2   3

Over-All Impressions:

- Adhered to time requirements/restrictions   0   1   2   3
- Appeared prepared and practiced   0   1   2   3
- Dressed appropriately   0   1   2   3
- Used extemporaneous delivery   0   1   2   3

Comments:

Best aspects of speech (name at least two):

Areas for improvement:

Persuasive Speech Critique

0 Not Provided	1 Below Expectations	2 Meets Expectations	3 Exceeds Expectations

Speech Content

Introduction:

• Grabbed audience's attention	0	1	2	3
• Established credibility/speaker's link	0	1	2	3
• Linked audience to topic	0	1	2	3
• Revealed position on issue	0	1	2	3
• Previewed main points/central idea	0	1	2	3

Body:

• Provided adequate support materials/evidence	0	1	2	3
• Orally cited appropriate sources (minimum 3)	0	1	2	3
• Organized effectively	0	1	2	3
• Provided smooth transitions	0	1	2	3

Conclusion:

• Had "brakelight" (signaled the end)	0	1	2	3
• Reviewed main points	0	1	2	3
• Ended with strong clincher	0	1	2	3
• Issued specific appeal or challenge	0	1	2	3

Visual Aids:

• Relevant to speech	0	1	2	3
• Easy to see/read	0	1	2	3
• Presented effectively	0	1	2	3
• Followed professional guidelines	0	1	2	3

Speaker's Name _____

Class Time _____

Persuasive Speech Critique

0 Not Provided	1 Below Expectations	2 Meets Expectations	3 Exceeds Expectations

Speech Content

Introduction:

• Grabbed audience's attention	0	1	2	3
• Established credibility/speaker's link	0	1	2	3
• Linked audience to topic	0	1	2	3
• Revealed position on issue	0	1	2	3
• Previewed main points/central idea	0	1	2	3

Body:

• Provided adequate support materials/evidence	0	1	2	3
• Orally cited appropriate sources (minimum 3)	0	1	2	3
• Organized effectively	0	1	2	3
• Provided smooth transitions	0	1	2	3

Conclusion:

• Had "brakelight" (signaled the end)	0	1	2	3
• Reviewed main points	0	1	2	3
• Ended with strong clincher	0	1	2	3
• Issued specific appeal or challenge	0	1	2	3

Visual Aids:

• Relevant to speech	0	1	2	3
• Easy to see/read	0	1	2	3
• Presented effectively	0	1	2	3
• Followed professional guidelines	0	1	2	3

Speaker

Eye Contact:
- Looked at all parts of audience   0   1   2   3
- Referred to note cards appropriately   0   1   2   3

Gestures and Posture:
- Avoided distracting mannerisms   0   1   2   3
- Used effective/natural gestures   0   1   2   3
- Used appropriate facial expressions   0   1   2   3

Voice:
- Spoke at ideal rate   0   1   2   3
- Avoided awkward pauses   0   1   2   3
- Sounded energetic/sincere   0   1   2   3
- Spoke in a conversational tone   0   1   2   3

Wording:
- Pronounced words correctly   0   1   2   3
- Used correct grammar   0   1   2   3
- Used appropriate word choice   0   1   2   3
- Avoided verbal fillers (uh, um, er, okay, right, like, you know)   0   1   2   3

Over-All Impressions:
- Adhered to time requirements/restrictions   0   1   2   3
- Appeared prepared and practiced   0   1   2   3
- Dressed appropriately   0   1   2   3
- Used extemporaneous delivery   0   1   2   3

Comments:

Best aspects of speech (name at least two):

Areas for improvement:

Speaker

Eye Contact:
- Looked at all parts of audience   0   1   2   3
- Referred to note cards appropriately   0   1   2   3

Gestures and Posture:
- Avoided distracting mannerisms   0   1   2   3
- Used effective/natural gestures   0   1   2   3
- Used appropriate facial expressions   0   1   2   3

Voice:
- Spoke at ideal rate   0   1   2   3
- Avoided awkward pauses   0   1   2   3
- Sounded energetic/sincere   0   1   2   3
- Spoke in a conversational tone   0   1   2   3

Wording:
- Pronounced words correctly   0   1   2   3
- Used correct grammar   0   1   2   3
- Used appropriate word choice   0   1   2   3
- Avoided verbal fillers (uh, um, er, okay, right, like, you know)   0   1   2   3

Over-All Impressions:
- Adhered to time requirements/restrictions   0   1   2   3
- Appeared prepared and practiced   0   1   2   3
- Dressed appropriately   0   1   2   3
- Used extemporaneous delivery   0   1   2   3

Comments:

Best aspects of speech (name at least two):

Areas for improvement:

Persuasive Speech Critique

0 Not Provided	1 Below Expectations	2 Meets Expectations	3 Exceeds Expectations

Speech Content

Introduction:

• Grabbed audience's attention	0	1	2	3
• Established credibility/speaker's link	0	1	2	3
• Linked audience to topic	0	1	2	3
• Revealed position on issue	0	1	2	3
• Previewed main points/central idea	0	1	2	3

Body:

• Provided adequate support materials/evidence	0	1	2	3
• Orally cited appropriate sources (minimum 3)	0	1	2	3
• Organized effectively	0	1	2	3
• Provided smooth transitions	0	1	2	3

Conclusion:

• Had "brakelight" (signaled the end)	0	1	2	3
• Reviewed main points	0	1	2	3
• Ended with strong clincher	0	1	2	3
• Issued specific appeal or challenge	0	1	2	3

Visual Aids:

• Relevant to speech	0	1	2	3
• Easy to see/read	0	1	2	3
• Presented effectively	0	1	2	3
• Followed professional guidelines	0	1	2	3

Speaker's Name _____

Class Time _____

Persuasive Speech Critique

0 Not Provided	1 Below Expectations	2 Meets Expectations	3 Exceeds Expectations

Speech Content

Introduction:

• Grabbed audience's attention	0	1	2	3
• Established credibility/speaker's link	0	1	2	3
• Linked audience to topic	0	1	2	3
• Revealed position on issue	0	1	2	3
• Previewed main points/central idea	0	1	2	3

Body:

• Provided adequate support materials/evidence	0	1	2	3
• Orally cited appropriate sources (minimum 3)	0	1	2	3
• Organized effectively	0	1	2	3
• Provided smooth transitions	0	1	2	3

Conclusion:

• Had "brakelight" (signaled the end)	0	1	2	3
• Reviewed main points	0	1	2	3
• Ended with strong clincher	0	1	2	3
• Issued specific appeal or challenge	0	1	2	3

Visual Aids:

• Relevant to speech	0	1	2	3
• Easy to see/read	0	1	2	3
• Presented effectively	0	1	2	3
• Followed professional guidelines	0	1	2	3

Speaker

Eye Contact:
- Looked at all parts of audience 0 1 2 3
- Referred to note cards appropriately 0 1 2 3

Gestures and Posture:
- Avoided distracting mannerisms 0 1 2 3
- Used effective/natural gestures 0 1 2 3
- Used appropriate facial expressions 0 1 2 3

Voice:
- Spoke at ideal rate 0 1 2 3
- Avoided awkward pauses 0 1 2 3
- Sounded energetic/sincere 0 1 2 3
- Spoke in a conversational tone 0 1 2 3

Wording:
- Pronounced words correctly 0 1 2 3
- Used correct grammar 0 1 2 3
- Used appropriate word choice 0 1 2 3
- Avoided verbal fillers (uh, um, er, okay, right, like, you know) 0 1 2 3

Over-All Impressions:
- Adhered to time requirements/restrictions 0 1 2 3
- Appeared prepared and practiced 0 1 2 3
- Dressed appropriately 0 1 2 3
- Used extemporaneous delivery 0 1 2 3

Comments:

Best aspects of speech (name at least two):

Areas for improvement:

Speaker

Eye Contact:
- Looked at all parts of audience 0 1 2 3
- Referred to note cards appropriately 0 1 2 3

Gestures and Posture:
- Avoided distracting mannerisms 0 1 2 3
- Used effective/natural gestures 0 1 2 3
- Used appropriate facial expressions 0 1 2 3

Voice:
- Spoke at ideal rate 0 1 2 3
- Avoided awkward pauses 0 1 2 3
- Sounded energetic/sincere 0 1 2 3
- Spoke in a conversational tone 0 1 2 3

Wording:
- Pronounced words correctly 0 1 2 3
- Used correct grammar 0 1 2 3
- Used appropriate word choice 0 1 2 3
- Avoided verbal fillers (uh, um, er, okay, right, like, you know) 0 1 2 3

Over-All Impressions:
- Adhered to time requirements/restrictions 0 1 2 3
- Appeared prepared and practiced 0 1 2 3
- Dressed appropriately 0 1 2 3
- Used extemporaneous delivery 0 1 2 3

Comments:

Best aspects of speech (name at least two):

Areas for improvement: